Activity Workbook
ExpressWays
Second Edition

Steven J. Molinsky
Bill Bliss

Contributing Author
Dorothy Lynde

PRENTICE HALL REGENTS
A VIACOM COMPANY

Publisher: *Louisa B. Hellegers*
Electronic Production Editor: *Carey Davies*
Manufacturing Manager: *Ray Keating*

Electronic Art Production Supervision: *Todd Ware*
Electronic Art Production/Scanning: *Marita Froimson*
Art Director: *Merle Krumper*
Interior Design: *Ken Liao*

Illustrator: *Richard Hill*

The authors gratefully acknowledge the contribution of Tina Carver
in the development of the *ExpressWays* program.

PRENTICE HALL REGENTS
A VIACOM COMPANY

© 1997 by PRENTICE HALL REGENTS
Prentice-Hall, Inc.
A Simon & Schuster Company
Upper Saddle River, New Jersey 07458

10   9   8   7   6   5   4   3

ISBN   0-13-570896-6

Prentice-Hall International (UK) Limited, *London*
Prentice-Hall of Australia Pty. Limited, *Sydney*
Prentice-Hall Canada Inc., *Toronto*
Prentice-Hall Hispanoamericana, S.A., *Mexico*
Prentice-Hall of India Private Limited, *New Delhi*
Prentice-Hall of Japan, Inc., *Tokyo*
Simon & Schuster Asia Pte. Ltd., *Singapore*
Editora Prentice-Hall do Brasil, Ltda., *Rio de Janeiro*

EXPRESSWAYS 3
Activity Workbook
TRAVEL GUIDE

Exit 3 • People and Places

Exit 4 • Housing and Food

Exit 5 • At Work

Exit 6 • Health and Emergencies

Greet Someone and Introduce Yourself

A. The Right Choice

Circle the correct words.

A. You're new here, (aren't you) / you aren't [1] ?

B. Yes, I do / am [2] . My name is Ken Watson.

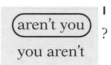

A. I name / I'm [3] Sue Potter. Nice to meet you.

B. Nice meeting you, too / Nice to meeting you, too [4] .

A. Tell me, which department are you working / do you work in [5] ?

B. Shipping. What are you / What about you [6] ?

A. Accounting.

B. Listen

Listen and circle the word you hear.

1 (Which)	What	3 What	Whose	5 Who	Whose
2 Whose	Who	4 How	Who	6 Why	What

1

C. Wrong Way!

Put the lines in the correct order.

___ Hello. I'm Rosa Gomez. Nice to meet you.

_1_ Hello. Let me introduce myself. I'm your neighbor. My name is Barry Burns.

___ Nice meeting you, too. Tell me, what floor do you live on?

___ The 4th.

___ The 9th. And you?

D. What's the Response?

Choose the correct response.

1 Where are you from?
   a. English.
   b. England. *(circled)*

2 Who is your neighbor?
   a. I don't know.
   b. I'm a good neighbor.

3 When did you move in?
   a. Next Tuesday.
   b. Yesterday.

4 I'm enjoying my new job. How about you?
   a. I have some good days and some bad days.
   b. You do.

5 Whose class are you in?
   a. Spanish.
   b. Mr. Cramer's.

6 How are you enjoying your new neighbors?
   a. On Mondays for dinner.
   b. They're very nice.

7 Why are you here?
   a. I came to study accounting.
   b. I moved in two weeks ago.

8 What floor do you live on?
   a. 8B.
   b. The 8th.

9 Which department do you work in?
   a. The 7th.
   b. Personnel.

10 Tell me, how are you enjoying your classes?
   a. Oh, they have their ups and downs.
   b. Accounting and History.

11 Which apartment do you live in?
   a. 6D.
   b. It's small.

12 I'm a mechanic at Al's Garage. How about you?
   a. How do you do?
   b. I work at the library.

2

E. The Right Choice

Circle the correct word.

1 A. When (do (did)) you move in?
   B. Two weeks ago.

2 A. (Do Am) I going to be okay,
     Dr. DiMarco?
   B. You're going to be fine.

3 A. When (do are) you start classes?
   B. Next week.

4 A. How (is are) you enjoying
     school?
   B. I like it a lot.

5 A. (Is Does) your son have a car?
   B. No. He has a motorcycle.

6 A. When (is do) the new tenant
     going to move in?
   B. I'm not sure.

7 A. (Do Are) you sure?
   B. I'm positive!

8 A. (Do Is) your teachers give a
     lot of homework?
   B. Yes. We have homework every day.

F. Listen

Listen and decide what they're talking about.

1 (transportation) housing   **4** health housing   **7** health school

2 housing work   **5** work housing   **8** transportation work

3 work school   **6** health work   **9** housing work

G. WordRap: *Meeting People*

Listen. Then clap and practice.

A. You live here, don't you?
B. Yes, I do.
A. What's your name?
B. My name is Sue.

A. You're new here, aren't you?
B. Yes, I am.
A. What's your name?
B. My name is Sam.

A. You teach here, don't you?
B. Yes, I do.
A. Where's your class?
B. In Room 202.

A. You study here, don't you?
B. Yes, I do.
A. Who's your teacher?
B. Mr. Crew.

A. More Formal or Less Formal?

Decide whether the following are "more formal" or "less formal."

		More Formal	Less Formal
1	"How do you do?"	✓	
2	"How are you doing?"		
3	"I'd like you to meet my husband, Vincent."		
4	"This is my son, Billy."		
5	"How are things?"		
6	"Let me introduce you to my father, Mr. Sanchez."		
7	"I'd like to introduce my mother-in-law, Mrs. Ames."		
8	"Hi."		

B. Listen

Listen and choose the correct people.

1 ✓ ___   2 ___ ___   3 ___ ___

4 ___ ___   5 ___ ___   6 ___ ___

C. Wrong Way!

Put the words in the correct order.

1 doing?   are   How   you
   How are you doing?

2 things?   How   are
   _____

3 my   I'd   Jane.   to   introduce   wife,   like
   _____

4 you.   meeting   It's   nice
   _____

Give Information About Countries and Nationalities

A. Wrong Way!

Put the lines in the correct order.

1

___ Colombian?

___ Where in Colombia are you from?

_1_ Passport, please!

___ I'm not surprised. A lot of Colombians are on vacation at this time of year.

___ Yes.

___ Bogotá.

___ Here you are.

___ There sure are a lot of people from Colombia visiting right now.

2

_1_ How long do you plan to stay?

___ Thank you.

___ Next!

___ All right. Here's your passport. Welcome to the United States.

___ About three weeks.

B. Matching Lines

Match the lines.

_e_ **1** Are you Australian?   a. Florence.

___ **2** What's your favorite food?   b. I don't know yet.

___ **3** Do you speak Vietnamese?   c. Is Kyoto in Japan?

___ **4** What's your favorite Canadian city?   d. Yes. I'm from Rio de Janeiro.

___ **5** I'm going to travel to Kyoto soon.   e. No. I'm South African.

___ **6** Is Seoul a city in China?   f. No. It's in Korea.

___ **7** Where in Italy are you from?   g. Sushi.

___ **8** Are you Brazilian?   h. Montreal.

___ **9** Where are you going on vacation?   i. Just a little.

5

C. Crosswalk

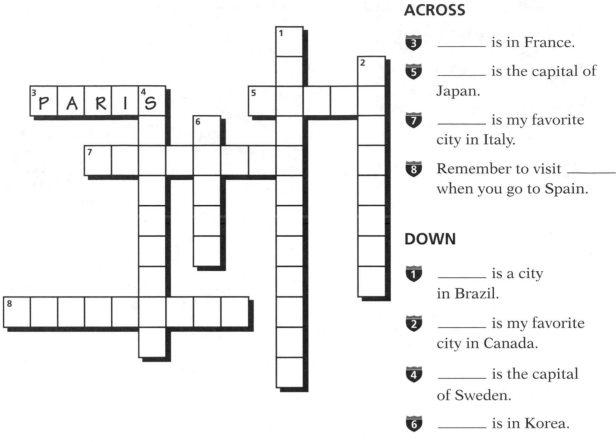

ACROSS

3 _____ is in France.

5 _____ is the capital of Japan.

7 _____ is my favorite city in Italy.

8 Remember to visit _____ when you go to Spain.

DOWN

1 _____ is a city in Brazil.

2 _____ is my favorite city in Canada.

4 _____ is the capital of Sweden.

6 _____ is in Korea.

D. Listen

Listen and circle the correct word.

1	(Italian)	Italy	4	Spaniard	Spanish	7	French	France
2	Japan	Japanese	5	Brazilian	Brazil	8	Spanish	Colombian
3	Swedes	Swedish	6	Korean	Korea	9	Canadian	French

E. Open Road!

Tell about yourself.

1 What's your favorite country to visit? ....

2 Why do you like to go there? ....

3 What languages do you speak? ....

4 Where did you go on your last vacation? ....

5 Where are you going on your next vacation? ....

A. The Right Choice

Circle the correct words.

A. May I help you?

B. Yes. I have a [respiration / **reservation**]¹.

A. [Whose / **What's**]² your last name?

B. Spencer.

A. Could you [say / **spell**]³ that, please?

B. S–P–E–N–C–E–R.

A. [**First** / Front]⁴ name Veronica?

B. That's [collect / **correct**]⁵.

A. I see here you [**requested** / connected]⁶ twin beds.

B. [Not ready / Not really]⁷. I requested a king-size bed.

A. Oh. I guess we had the wrong information in the computer. [No people / No problem]⁸.

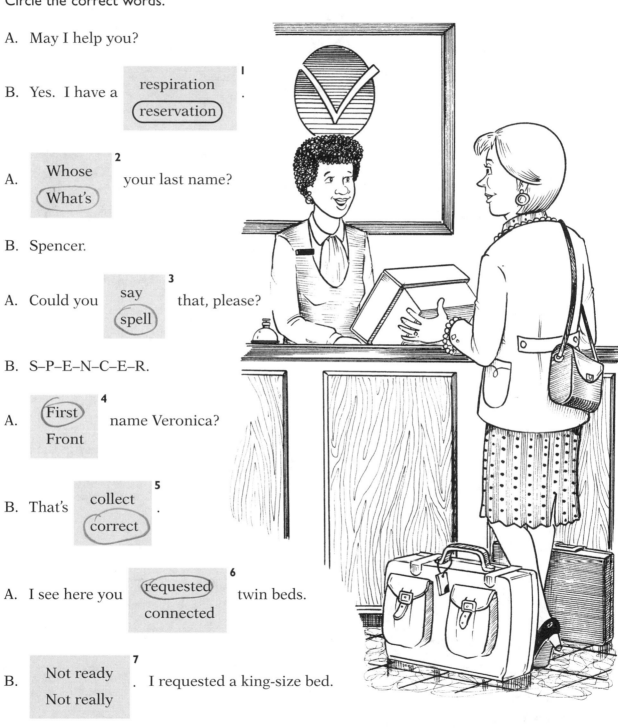

B. What's the Word?

Complete the sentences.

| reservation | facing | suite | alone | bed | charging | staying | check in |

1. My name is Harold Baines, and I have a ___reservation___.

2. According to our records, you requested a _____.

3. I'll be _____ for two nights.

4. Are you _____ your bill to American Express?

5. I requested a king-size _____.

6. Are you traveling _____ or with your family?

7. I asked for a room _____ the park.

8. You need to _____ at the front desk.

C. Listen

Listen and choose the correct response.

1. (a.) Yes. I have a reservation.
   b. Yes. I'll help you.

2. a. That's correct.
   b. Not really.

3. a. I'm traveling by bus.
   b. I'm traveling with my family.

4. a. Yes. I'm checking in.
   b. No. I'm charging my bill.

5. a. No. I requested a reservation.
   b. No, actually not. I requested a suite.

6. a. Three days.
   b. I'm staying with my family.

7. a. That's right.
   b. I asked for a check facing the park.

8. a. Could you spell that, please?
   b. And your last name?

D. Open Road!

This hotel has the wrong information about your reservation. Complete the conversation any way you wish.

A. I'm sorry, but we don't have your request for a suite in our computer.

B. ....

A. ....

B. ....

A. ....

B. ....

A. Open Road!

You hurt yourself! What do you say at the hospital?

A. Before the doctor sees you, we need some information. What's your last name?

B. _Vazquez_

A. Could you spell that, please?

B. _V, A, Z, Q, U, E, Z_

A. And your first name?

B _Edmundo_

A. Address?

B. _14725 TITUS ST #6_

A. Telephone number?

B. _(818) 779-00-41_

A. What's your date of birth?

B. _(03-01-85)_

A. And what's your Social Security number?

B. ....

A. Do you have medical insurance?

B. _Not_

A. Do you know the I.D. number?

B. ....

A. Take a seat over there, and somebody will see you in a few minutes.

B. What's the Question?

Complete the conversations.

1 _What's your apartment number_ ?
4C.

2 _Wht is your Thelephone umber_
(902) 559-2375.

3 _Do you Know The I.D. Number._
02246.

4 _what's your date of birth_ ?
12/4/72.

C. What Are They Saying?

What are these people expressing?

Hello.

1 This person is _____.
  a. greeting someone *(circled)*
  b. asking for information

This is my wife, Carol.

2 This person is _____.
  a. asking for information
  b. introducing someone *(circled)*

How do you do?

3 This person is _____.
  a. correcting someone
  b. greeting someone *(circled)*

Could you spell that?

4 This person is _____.
  a. asking for information *(circled)*
  b. giving information

How are you doing?

5 This person is _____.
  a. introducing someone
  b. greeting someone *(circled)*

What are you doing?

6 This person is _____.
  a. greeting someone
  b. asking for information *(circled)*

D. Analogies

student	Not really.	university	work	telephone number
came	Biology	difficult	This is Tom.	in a little while

1 How do you do? : Hi! *as* Let me introduce you to Tom. : _____This is Tom._____

2 live : apartment *as* study : ___Biology___

3 supervisor : worker *as* teacher : _____

4 have : had *as* come : _____

5 late : early *as* easy : _____

6 move in : apartment *as* major in : _____

7 yes : That's correct. *as* no : _____

8 zip code : address *as* area code : _____

9 why : because it snowed *as* when : _____

10 passport number : travel *as* Social Security number : _____

E. Word Search

Find the names of 10 family members.

```
R  I  P  D  G  S  L  O  U  T  L  S  I  F  Z  B  B  O  P
D  L  E  B  A  I  J  Y  L  X  H  W  P  L  L  A  W  A  Y
A  O  K  E  Q  S  A  C  T  P  H  R  A  W  L  N  C  M  M
U  E  R  P  U  T (S  O  N) G  S  L  Q  O  D  G  K  U  O
G  T  C  S  E  A  N  A  F  A  T  H  U  P  B  U  O  U  T
H  E  P  H  E  K  U  P  A  N  N  S  N  P  R  N  P  K  H
T  L  O  P  X  E  P  T  A  I  O  P  E  P  O  P  L  Z  E
E  Y  W  R  Y  O  P  G  H  E  P  S  P  H  T  Z  C  B  R
R  Q  E  T  U  U  P  A  A  C  S  C  H  T (H  O  W) N  P
W  I  V  E  T  M  A  F  A  E  H  I  E  F  E (W  I  F  E)
H (B  R  O  T  H  E  R  S) D  A  H  W  A  G  N  E  I  C
M  O  T  H  E  E  R  W  O  D  A  U  G  H  T  S  U  N  N
N  S  I  S  T  E  R  C  O  E  Y  S  B  R  T  T  A  U
A  D  G  J  K  R  L  X  N  N  W  B  T  U  O  S  P  A  G
N  K  L  D  S  O  Y  N  G  L  X  A  W  Y  O  N  C  P  C
U  C  L  A  L  K  E  M  U  T  D  N  W  P  A  W  A  E  J
P  U  T (F  A  T  H  E  R  S) V  D  W  R  D  E  W  P  P
```

F. Matching Lines

Match the situations.

_h_	**1** "Hi."	a. Asking about a course
___	**2** "How do you do?"	b. Asking about a boss
___	**3** "When did you move in?"	c. Checking in at a hotel
___	**4** "What days does it meet?"	d. Meeting in a formal situation
___	**5** "Do you have medical insurance?"	e. Asking about a teacher
___	**6** "Which department do you work in?"	f. Talking to a new neighbor
_c_	**7** "Do you have a reservation?"	g. Going through customs
___	**8** "Does he give a lot of tests?"	h. Meeting in an informal situation
_b_	**9** "Who is your supervisor?"	i. Meeting someone at work
___	**10** "How long do you plan to stay in this country?"	j. Giving information at the hospital

G. Open Road!

Complete the following any way you wish and then compare with a classmate.

1 What questions do you ask a new neighbor?

....

....

....

2 What questions do you ask a new co-worker?

....

....

....

3 What questions do they ask when you register for a course?

....

....

....

4 What questions do they ask when you go through customs?

....

....

....

5 What does the hotel clerk ask when you register at a hotel?

....

....

....

6 What do they ask when you go to the hospital emergency room?

....

....

....

Tell About Past Events

A. What's the Response?

Choose the correct response.

1. I just got a big promotion.
   a. Congratulations!
   b. I'm so sorry.

2. You seem upset. Is anything wrong?
   a. Yes, it's wrong.
   b. Yes, there is.

3. I have some bad news.
   a. Did you break up with Alice?
   b. Did you win the lottery?

4. That's fantastic!
   a. I think so, too.
   b. How about you?

5. I didn't receive any birthday presents.
   a. Is anything wrong?
   b. I'm very sorry to hear that.

6. All my plants died while I was away!
   a. What a shame!
   b. Why a shame!

7. What's new with you?
   a. How about you?
   b. Nothing much.

8. I didn't get the raise I was hoping for.
   a. That's a shame!
   b. That's great!

9. What's happening with you?
   a. I'm happening.
   b. Nothing much.

10. I have some good news.
    a. Did you pass your driver's test?
    b. Did you fail your driver's test?

11. I don't feel very well today.
    a. That's too bad!
    b. That's wonderful!

12. What's wrong?
    a. I have some good news.
    b. I have some bad news.

B. Listen

Listen and decide if it's "good news" or "bad news."

1. Good News    Bad News
2. Good News   Bad News
3. Good News   Bad News
4. Good News   Bad News
5. Good News   Bad News

6. Good News   Bad News
7. Good News   Bad News
8. Good News   Bad News
9. Good News   Bad News
10. Good News   Bad News

C. The Right Choice

Circle the correct word.

1. My husband (make (made)) me a cake for my birthday this year.

2. My friends (left   leave) work early today. I wonder why!

3. My mother-in-law (take   took) a plane to Miami last week.

4. I'm really hungry! I (ate   didn't eat) breakfast this morning.

5. Last month I (went   go) to Brazil on vacation. It was great!

6. Do you remember Bob Bennett? I (see   saw) him yesterday.

7. Joe didn't go to work today. He (felt   didn't feel) well.

8. I (got   get) my husband a tie for his birthday this year.

9. I have some bad news! I (didn't win   won) the lottery yesterday.

10. I looked for my keys in the office, but I (found   didn't find) them.

11. I have some good news. I finally (didn't get   got) a job yesterday!

12. I'm sorry you (didn't buy   bought) that blue sweater. It was beautiful!

13. I (wrote   write) to my parents last week to tell them about my new apartment.

14. Susie forgot her homework yesterday. I (have to   had to) take it to her at school.

D. WordRap: *Bad News!*

Listen. Then clap and practice.

A. What happened to Tad?
   He looks so sad.
B. He lost his job.
A. That's too bad!

A. What's wrong with Mame?
   She looks the same.
B. Her goldfish died.
A. What a shame!

A. What's wrong with Dad?
   He looks so mad.
B. His car was stolen.
A. That's too bad!

A. What's wrong with Sue?
   She looks so blue.
B. Her rent went up.
A. Mine did, too.

E. Greeting Card Match

Match the cards.

a.

b.

c.

d.

e.

f.

g.

h.

1 _c_ *Good luck with your new car!*

2 ___ Wishing you 50 more years of happiness!

3 ___ Congratulations on your new job!

4 ___ *Hope you get well soon!*

5 ___ Best wishes for a special 8-year-old!

6 ___ Wishing the new graduate a happy future!

7 ___ *Be happy as you start your life together!*

8 ___ Congratulations on the new arrival!

F. Open Road!

Write your own greeting for a special occasion.

....

....

....

Talk with Friends, Neighbors, and Co-workers

A. The Right Choice

Circle the correct word.

A. Henry?

B. Yes?

A. Can I [asked / **ask**]¹ you a question?

B. Sure. [What / Why]² ?

A. [Do / Did]³ the boss [fire / fired]⁴ his secretary this morning?

B. No. The boss didn't [fires / fire]⁵ his secretary. Where [do / did]⁶ you [hear / heard]⁷ that?

A. I [hear / heard]⁸ it in the cafeteria.

B. Well, I can't [believed / believe]⁹ it's true. I'm sure [its / it's]¹⁰ just a rumor.

B. Open Road!

Tell about a rumor you heard.

C. Listen

Listen and write the number under the correct picture.

___

___

___

1

___

___

___

___

D. The Right Choice

Circle the correct word.

1. Can I (tell (ask)) you a question?
2. Our supervisor (wents wants) to shorten our coffee break.
3. Someone mentioned it at the bus (driver stop).
4. I think the (boss loss) is going to fire me.
5. The taxi drivers plan to go on (fight strike) at midnight.
6. I can't believe it's (true false). I'm sure it's just a rumor.
7. The (apartment people) across the hall are getting a divorce.
8. (When Who) did you hear that?
9. He (heard beard) it at the office.
10. Our gym teacher (saw was) in the Olympics.
11. The whole school is (talking waking) about it!
12. (When Who) told you that?
13. I (told overheard) some people talking about it.
14. Our English teacher is going to (hit quit).
15. I didn't (receive believe) any birthday cards this year!
16. They were talking about it at our (union onion) meeting.

E. What's the Line?

Complete the conversations.

1 A. I hear the Apex Corporation wants to buy our company.
B. No. They ___don't want___ to buy OUR company.
They ___want___ to buy the company across the street.

2 A. Is our supervisor going to quit?
B. No. Our supervisor ___is it going___ to quit.
I think it's just a rumor.

3 A. I hear that Roger is getting a divorce.
B. That's not true. He ___is it getting___ a divorce.
___his is getting___ married!

4 A. Does the boss plan to lay off the managers?
B. No. She ___doesn't plan___ to lay off the managers. But I think she
___plants___ to lay off some of the secretaries.

5 A. Are the workers going to have to take a pay cut?
B. No. They ___aren't going___ to have to take a pay cut. Where did you hear that?

6 A. I hear that Melissa wants to leave the company.
B. That's not true. She ___doesn't want___ to leave the company. She
___She wants___ to take a vacation.

7 A. Is it true that sales were bad this month?
B. Where did you hear that? Sales ___weren't___ bad this month. In fact, they
___work___ very good!

F. Yes or No?

Is it a rumor? Check Yes or No.

		Yes	No
1	"The teachers are going on strike. I heard it on the radio."		✓
2	"The boss is planning to lay us off. I heard it in the cafeteria."	✓	
3	"I overheard in the elevator that we're all getting raises."	✓	
4	"Ten airline pilots just quit. I heard it on the 6 o'clock news."		✓
5	"Mrs. Fleming was in the Olympics. I saw her gold medal."		✓
6	"Someone told me the bookkeeper won the lottery yesterday."	✓	
7	"A few people mentioned that we might have to take a cut in pay."	✓	
8	"The mayor wrecked his car last night. I read it in the paper."		✓
9	"Mike told me that one of the supervisors thinks they're planning to close the factory."	✓	

18

A. The Right Choice

Circle the correct words.

A. What are you **(going)** / go ¹ to do this weekend?

B. My wife and I am going / **(are going)** ² to have a birthday party for our daughter.

A. A birthday party for your daughter?! We're / You're ³ certainly going / go ⁴ to be busy!

B. I suppose so. Now / How ⁵ about you? What is / are ⁶ YOUR plans for the weekend?

A. I don't know for sure. I'm pretty sure I'll be going / go ⁷ to the beach.

B. Well, have / do ⁸ a good weekend!

A. You, too / do ⁹ .

B. Open Road!

Tell about YOUR weekend plans.

I would like to go visit may uncle
an I need to fix may car.

C. What's the Question?

Complete the questions.

When	Where	What	How many	Why	Who

1. A. _____Where_____ are you going to plant those flowers?
   B. I'm going to plant them in my garden.

2. A. _____When_____ are you going to repaint your bedroom?
   B. I'm going to repaint it this summer.

3. A. _____What_____ are you going to do this weekend?
   B. I'm going to finish my term paper.

4. A. __How many__ friends are coming to your party?
   B. About 20 friends are coming.

5. A. _____Where_____ will you put these old photos?
   B. I'll put them in the attic.

6. A. _____Who_____ will tell the family the good news?
   B. Dad will tell everyone this weekend.

7. A. _____Why_____ are they going to lay off the workers?
   B. Because business isn't very good.

8. A. _____What_____ is your daughter going to do when she finishes school?
   B. She's going to look for a job as an accountant.

9. A. _____When_____ will you tell your parents you're getting married?
   B. I think I'll tell them this weekend.

D. Function Check

What are these people expressing?

1. "I'm going to see a movie."   (a.) certainty   b. uncertainty
2. "I'm not positive."   a. certainty   (b.) uncertainty
3. "I'll probably clean my house."   a. probability   (b.) improbability
4. "I'll most likely see a movie."   (a.) probability   b. improbability
5. "I'm pretty sure I'll come."   (a.) probability   b. improbability
6. "I don't know for sure."   a. certainty   (b.) uncertainty
7. "I'll be there at three o'clock."   (a.) certainty   b. uncertainty
8. "I promise I'll finish the report today." (a.) certainty   b. probability

E. Listen

Listen and number the activities.

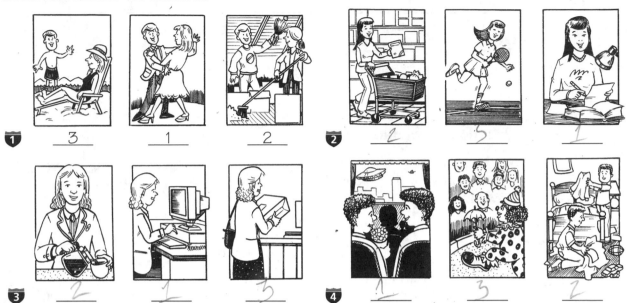

1 ___3___   ___1___   ___2___   2 ___2___   ___3___   ___1___

3 ___2___   ___1___   ___3___   4 ___1___   ___3___   ___2___

F. Crosswalk

ACROSS

2. Many people do _____ at home on the weekend.

4. You end a marriage when you get a _____.

5. A good place to go when it's hot is the _____.

7. When you paint a second time, you _____.

DOWN

1. People plant flowers in a _____.

2. Children love to go to the _____.

3. You can ask your boss for a _____.

6. Before people get married, they get _____.

7. I heard a _____ at work. I don't think it's true.

8. I'm going to a birthday _____.

21

A. Wrong Way!

Put the lines in the correct order.

1

___2___ Gee . . . uh. I don't know where to begin. What do you want to know?

___4___ No, I'm originally from Sante Fe. I was born there, I grew up there, and I went to school there. How about you?

___1___ So, tell me a little about yourself.

___3___ Well . . . Are you originally from around here?

___5___ I was born right here in New York and lived here until I finished high school.

2

___5___ I'm a lawyer. And you?

___3___ I have two brothers. They both live in Bangkok.

___6___ I'm a doctor.

___4___ In Bangkok? That's interesting. By the way, what do you do?

___7___ A doctor? That's interesting.

___2___ Yes. I have three brothers and a sister. They all live in Los Angeles. How about you?

___1___ Tell me about your family. Do you have any brothers and sisters?

B. Listen

Listen and choose the correct response.

1
a. I don't know where to begin.
b. Do you know?

2
a. Do you generally live here?
b. Are you originally from around here?

3
a. I'm from Cleveland.
b. Nice to meet you.

4
a. No, I'm not.
b. Yes, I do.

5
a. I have a brother and a sister.
b. By the way.

6
a. Yes. I have three sisters.
b. No. I'm not married.

7
a. I don't.
b. I'm an accountant.

8
a. I'm a teacher.
b. That's interesting.

C. Open Road!

Tell a little about yourself and your family.

We are tree brother and 3 sister

We are from mexico

D. What's the Word?

Complete the following.

invite	buying	see	do	relax	visit	wash	sleep
rake	prepare	look	go	read	eat	spend	

Many people _____look_____ ¹ forward to the weekend. They like to enjoy themselves and have fun. On Friday nights, many people like to ____relax____ ² at home after work and watch TV. Other people _____go_____ ³ out for dinner or go to _____see_____ ⁴ a movie.

On Saturdays, supermarkets and shopping malls are crowded with people __buying__ ⁵ food, clothing, or presents. Many people _____ ⁶ chores around the house on Saturday. They paint, _____ ⁷ leaves, _____ ⁸ their cars, and do laundry. On Saturday evenings, many people go out, _____ ⁹ people to come over for dinner, or _____ ¹⁰ friends.

On Sunday mornings, many people _____ ¹¹ late. Some people go to church, _____ ¹² the newspaper, and _____ ¹³ Sunday "brunch." On Sunday afternoons, many people have a big dinner and visit relatives. Other people _____ ¹⁴ Sunday afternoons at museums, theaters, and shopping malls. On Sunday evenings, people usually stay home and _____ ¹⁵ for the week ahead.

E. Listen

Listen and circle the word you hear.

1	(relax)	go back	**4**	chores	shores	**7**	visit	wish
2	father	brother	**5**	brush	brunch	**8**	watch	wash
3	day	play	**6**	zoo	soon	**9**	rock	lot

F. Matching Lines

Match the lines.

_d_	**1**	What's your favorite part of the week?	a. I'm a teacher.
_h_	**2**	Where did you grow up?	b. Sure. What?
_i_	**3**	I won a prize at the county fair.	c. I visit friends and watch TV.
_f_	**4**	My daughter broke up with her fiancé.	d. The weekend.
_a_	**5**	What do you do?	e. I heard it in the cafeteria.
_j_	**6**	Tell me about your family.	f. What a shame!
_g_	**7**	Are you positive?	g. Yes, I am.
_e_	**8**	Who told you that?	h. In Chicago.
_b_	**9**	Can I ask you something?	i. That's great!
_c_	**10**	What do you usually do to relax on the weekend?	j. I have one sister and three brothers.

G. Wrong Way!

Harry had an incredible weekend. What happened? Put the words in the correct order.

1 married On he afternoon girlfriend. his Friday

Friday afternoon he married on girlfried

2 lottery. they Saturday won the On in $10,000

_____

H. Open Road!

Tell about YOUR weekend.

....

....

Call Directory Assistance

A. Wrong Way!

Put the lines in the correct order.

____ Can you spell that?

____ Hmm. I'm pretty sure, but I'd better check.
Thank you, Operator.

____ What street?

__1__ Directory assistance. What city?

____ Just a moment. . . . I'm sorry, but I don't have
a Carl Morrison on Alamo Road. Are you
certain you have the correct address?

____ M-O-R-R-I-S-O-N.

____ Alamo Road.

____ Dallas. I'd like the number of Carl Morrison.

B. Fill It In!

Fill in the correct answer.

1 Directory assistance. _____?
  a. What street?
  b. What city? *(b circled)*

2 I'd like the number of _____.
  a. Middle Street
  b. Michael Gonzalez

3 Just a moment . . . _____.
  a. The number is 223-6710.
  b. The address is 45 Lantern Lane.

4 Are you certain you _____?
  a. have the correct number
  b. have the correct address

5 I'm pretty sure, but _____.
  a. I'd better check
  b. I'd better chest

6 Thank you, _____.
  a. Operation
  b. Operator

7 I'm sorry, but _____.
  a. I don't know a Joe Day at B Street
  b. I don't have a Joe Day on B Street

25

C. Listen

Listen and put a check next to the sentence you hear.

1 ✓ I hear about it every day.
    ___ I heard about it every day.

5 ___ That telephone number is long!
    ___ That telephone number is wrong!

2 ___ Go to the corner and turn at the light.
    ___ Go to the corner and turn right.

6 ___ She wants to go to work tomorrow.
    ___ She won't go to work tomorrow.

3 ___ I walk to the store every day.
    ___ I work at the store every day.

7 ___ That teacher taught math.
    ___ That teacher thought about math.

4 ___ Do you have any plants?
    ___ Do you have any plans?

8 ___ Sally won the race.
    ___ Sally was number eight.

D. Open Road!

Complete the conversation any way you wish.

A. Directory assistance. What city?

    ....

B. I'd like the number of ....

A. Would you spell that?

B. ....

A. What street?

B. ....

A. Just a moment. The number is ....

B. Thank you, Operator.

E. Listen

Listen and write the spelling of each name.

1 L - A - W - L - E - R

4 ___-___-___-___-___-___

2 ___-___-___-___

5 ___-___-___-___-___

3 ___-___-___-___

6 ___-___-___-___-___-___

A. The Right Choice

Circle the correct word.

A. Hello.

B. Hello. Dr. Ableman?

A. I'm [sure / **sorry**]¹. There's [nobody / somebody]² here by that [number / name]³.

B. Is [this / he]⁴ 396-1136?

A. No, it [is / isn't]⁵.

B. Oh. I [apologize / apology]⁶. I guess I [dial / dialed]⁷ the wrong number.

B. Matching Lines

Match the questions and answers.

_e_ **1** Is this 478-0092?   a. No, I don't.

___ **2** Did they have a good day?   b. No, I'm not.

___ **3** Do you have good news?   c. No, they weren't.

___ **4** Are they from here?   d. No, it wasn't.

___ **5** Was it easy?   e. No, it isn't.

___ **6** Were your children at school yesterday?   f. No, he doesn't.

___ **7** Does Bill drive to work every day?   g. No, they aren't.

___ **8** Are you having trouble with this exercise?   h. No, they didn't.

27

C. What Are They Saying?

Choose the correct answer.

Can you spell that?

1 This person is _____.
  (a.) asking for
      information
  b. apologizing

Excuse me.

2 This person is _____.
  a. apologizing
  b. reporting
     information

What city?

3 This person is _____.
  a. certain
  b. asking for
     information

I'm positive.

4 This person is _____.
  a. certain
  b. uncertain

I'm sorry.

5 This person is _____.
  a. reporting
     information
  b. apologizing

I'm pretty sure.

6 This person is _____.
  a. almost positive
  b. not sure

D. Open Road!

Call a friend and report some good news.

A. Hello.

B. Hello, ...? This is ....
   I have some good news to tell you.

A. What?

B. ....

A. That's ....!

Call a friend and report some bad news.

A. Hello.

B. Hello, ...? This is ....
   I have some bad news to tell you.

A. What?

B. ....

A. That's ....!

A. The Right Choice

Circle the correct words.

A. Pardon me. Does this bus go to Las Vegas?

B. No, it (**doesn't** does)¹. It goes to Seattle. You want the Nevada bus.

A. The Nevada bus?

B. (**Yes** No)².

A. (When **Where**)³ can I get it?

B. It's at (pier **gate**)⁴ 7.

A. (**Thank you** Excuse me)⁵.

A. (**Excuse me** Thanks)⁶. Where can I get the 8:00 flight to Denver?

B. I'm (pardon **sorry**)⁷, but that flight just left.

A. (Oh, yes **Oh, no**)⁸! I missed the flight?!

B. I'm afraid you did.

A. I can't believe it! (I got to **I've got to**)⁹ get to a business meeting. When is the next flight?

B. (**Let me see** I don't believe)¹⁰. It's at 10:00. Will that get you to Denver in time for your business meeting?

A. (**I hope so** I need to)¹¹.

B. Sense or Nonsense?

Do each of the following "make sense" or are they "nonsense"?

		Sense	Nonsense
1	"You can get the ferry at pier 7."	✓	
2	"The bus to Washington is at gate 34."	✓	
3	"The express train is on the expressway."		✓
4	"This monorail goes to the parking lot."		✓
5	"I can't believe it! I missed my ticket!"	✓	
6	"You can buy your reunion right here."		✓

C. Crosswalk

ACROSS

5. I'm getting married. Today is my _____ day.

8. The _____ is at pier 4.

9. When I graduate from college, I'm going to my college _____.

10. Wait for the train on the other _____.

DOWN

1. I'm going to my high school _____.

2. The ship leaves from _____ 15.

3. I have bad news. I have to go to a _____.

4. This _____ goes to the Magic Kingdom.

6. Flight 754 leaves from _____ 2B.

7. The train to Las Vegas is on _____ 45.

D. WordRap: *Going Places!*

Listen. Then clap and practice.

A. Does this plane go to Timbuktu?
B. No, you want flight 402.

A. Does this bus stop in front of the store?
B. No, you want bus number 4.

A. Does this flight go to Santa Fe?
B. Yes, it does, but it's full today.

A. Is there a train to Idaho?
B. Yes, but it left an hour ago!

A. Where can I get bus 24?
B. Right over there, near the candy store.

A. Where can I find track number 3?
B. That's where I'm going. Just follow me.

A. The Right Choice

Circle the correct words.

A. Excuse me. (Could you tell me)[1] / Could you tell how to get to the City Park?

B. Yes. Drive down this road until you go to / get to [2] the next intersection. Turn right and drive two blocks. Turn left, and you'll see the park on the left.

A. I'm sorry. I didn't get that [3] / I didn't say that . Could you please remember / repeat [4] that?

B. Okay. First, go to the next car / corner [5] and turn right on Oak Street.

A. Okay.

B. Then drive two blocks, and turn left on Pine Street. Are you with me [6] / Are you follow me so far?

A. Yes. I don't understand [7] / understand .

B. You'll see the park on the left. Have you got all that?

A. Yes, now I got it [8] / I've got it . Thanks very much.

B. You're welcome.

B. The 5th Wheel!

Which one doesn't belong?

1	Okay.	Sure.	(I'm sorry.)	All right.
2	Excuse me.	I'm following you.	I'm with you.	I understand.
3	I apologize.	That's right.	Excuse me.	I'm sorry.
4	I've got to	I want to	I have to	I need to
5	Okay so far?	I didn't follow you.	I didn't get that.	I don't understand.
6	Are you there?	Can you tell me?	Do you know?	Could you tell me?
7	Are you sure?	Are you certain?	Are you positive?	Do you know?
8	Uh-húh.	I didn't follow you.	That's right.	Yes.

C. Listen

Look at the map and listen to the directions. If the directions are correct, write **C**. If they are incorrect, write **I**.

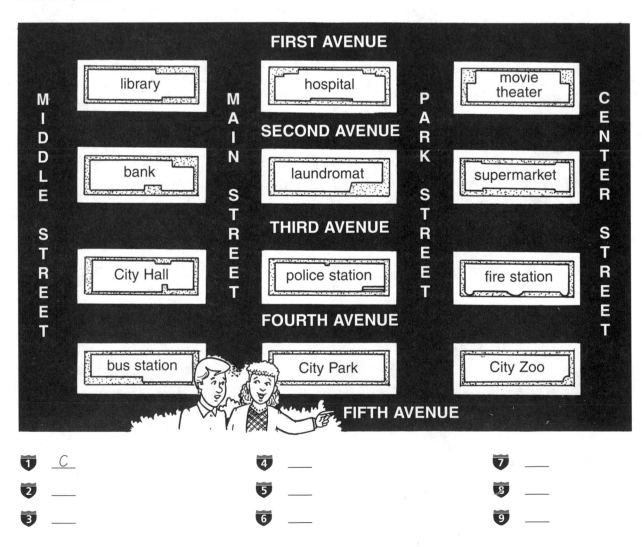

1	_C_	**4**	___	**7**	___
2	___	**5**	___	**8**	___
3	___	**6**	___	**9**	___

D. What's the Line?

Complete the conversation any way you wish.

A. <u>could you tell me</u> [1] how to get to the university?

B. Yes. Walk to the corner and turn right. Walk two blocks to Elm Street and turn left. Walk three more blocks, and you'll see the university on the left.

A. I'm sorry. I didn't get that. _____ [2] ?

B. Sure. First, walk to the corner and turn right.

A. _____ [3] .

B. Then walk two blocks to Elm Street and turn left. _____ [4] ?

A. Yes. I'm following you.

B. Then walk three more blocks, and you'll see the university on the left. Have you got all that?

A. Yes. <u>I got it</u> [5] . Thanks very much.

E. What's the Response?

Choose the correct response.

1 Excuse me. Do you know how to get to the park?
   a. Yes, there's a park.
   b. Yes, I do.

2 Go to the next corner and turn right.
   a. Turn the right corner?
   b. Turn at the next corner?

3 Yes. Turn right onto Oakland Avenue.
   a. Um-hmm.
   b. Do you repeat that?

4 Walk along Oakland Avenue a few blocks.
   a. Okay.
   b. I'll see.

5 You'll see the park on the left.
   a. I didn't know.
   b. On the left?

6 Yes. It's on the left, next to the museum.
   a. Park next to the museum?
   b. The park is next to the museum?

7 Yes. It's on the left, next to the museum.
   a. Now I'm with you.
   b. Now I'm so far.

8 Have you got all that?
   a. Yes. All right.
   b. Yes. Now I've got it.

A. Wrong Way!

Put the lines in the correct order.

___ Betty! Where ARE you?

___ Oh. That's the problem. You were supposed to get off at Exit 25.

___ I'm afraid I am.

_1_ Hello.

___ I think so. I took Maple Street to Fourth Avenue. Then I turned left and took the Interstate south to Exit 27.

___ You're lost?!

___ Tell me, Betty, where are you now?

_7_ Did you follow my directions?

___ Hello, Maria? This is Betty.

___ I'm calling from a phone at Denny's Donuts.

___ Exit 25?! Oh.

___ You won't believe it! I'm lost!

___ Oh, that's not far from here. Here's what you should do.

B. Matching Lines

Match the lines.

_b_ **1** Drive about three miles and you'll see a large ____.

___ **2** You'll see my house at the end of the ____.

___ **3** Follow Madison Street for two ____.

___ **4** Drive to the corner and turn ____.

___ **5** Take a right on Washington ____.

___ **6** You didn't follow my ____.

___ **7** Go north on the ____.

___ **8** Get off at Exit ____.

a. blocks
b. sign
c. interstate
d. directions
e. left
f. block
g. Boulevard
h. 15

C. What's the Word?

Complete the sentences.

commuters	honk	midday	rush	underground	carpools
intersection	hail	traffic	sites	highways	ancient

1 In Athens and Rome, they can't build new ___highways___ because of the historic sites.

2 In many cities, there are special lanes for _____ of three or more people.

3 The time of the day when people go to work and come home from work is called _____ hour.

4 In some countries, many workers go home for a _____ break.

5 Many people in Seoul stand at intersections and _____ a cab.

6 Some people _____ their horns when there is a lot of traffic.

7 The subway systems in Tokyo and Rome are _____.

8 The Forum and the Colosseum are historic _____.

9 The city streets are full of _____ at rush hour.

10 An _____ is the place where two streets meet.

11 Heavy _____ is a problem in many cities.

12 An old city is an _____ city.

D. The 5th Wheel!

Which one doesn't belong?

1 ancient | old | historic | (artifacts)

2 automobiles | mopeds | subways | city

3 carpool | highway | intersection | street

4 build | make | hail | construct

5 Athens | Canada | Seoul | Rome

6 archeologists | artifacts | ancient | normal

7 trains | packers | commuters | cab drivers

8 gate | track | moped | pier

9 ferry | pier | bus | plane

10 lunch | wedding | funeral | graduation

E. Word Search

Find 7 ways to get to and from work.

```
P D G C L O U T L S I F Z B B O
E B U C E S L X T A X Y W A Y A
T I B B I L T P H (T A X I S) C M
R P I T A R T O M O B O D G S U
C L C A N A W A T L U P B U O A
P I Y K U I A N N S V P T N P U
O P C E P M A U T O M A T I C T
W R L O P E B U S E S H K Z C O
E T E U P S A I S C U T D O W M
G J S R L X N N W E T U O S P O
L D R H Y N G L X Z W M O N C B
A E N L A Z Y O U B I O H A P I
X G S U B W A Y S U B P E D S L
P I D S G I V S E C I E S B U E
B B A Y H I G H W C C D F R G S
T R A I N S U T D O W S A W A T
```

F. Listen

Listen to the traffic report and choose the correct answers.

1
  a. There's an accident on the subway.
  (b.) There's an accident on the highway.

  c. Commuters should take the highway to work.
  (d.) Commuters should take the subway to work.

2
  a. The trains are very slow this morning.
  b. The buses are very fast this morning.

  c. Commuters should take the bus.
  d. Commuters should take taxis.

3
  a. It's snowing. The trains and buses are late.
  b. It's snowing. The trains and taxis are late.

  c. Getting to work will be difficult.
  d. Getting home from work will be difficult.

4
  a. There's good news for commuters today.
  b. There's good news for computers today.

  c. The new subway system is open.
  d. The new taxi system is open.

A. What's the Word?

Complete the sentences.

| Who | What | Where | When | Which | Why | Whose | How |

1. A. __What__ did you do last night?
   B. I invited people over for dinner.

2. A. _____ long are you going to stay?
   B. A few days.

3. A. _____ school do you go to?
   B. Burbank High School.

4. A. _____ understands the homework?
   B. Mary does.

5. A. _____ cake won first prize?
   B. Marvin Crawford's cake.

6. A. Excuse me. _____ is the ferry to Manhattan?
   B. It's at pier 7.

7. A. _____ is your birthday?
   B. It's July 15th.

8. A. _____ did they lay off the workers?
   B. There wasn't any work.

B. Listen

Listen and circle the word you hear.

1. (went)   want
2. wreck   wrecked
3. dial   dialed
4. find   found

5. heard   overheard
6. let   left
7. died   die
8. believed   believe

9. go   know
10. went   rent
11. heard   hear
12. gave   gives

C. Matching Lines

Match the lines.

__d__ 1. Is this 465-7798?

____ 2. Are you Greek?

____ 3. Could you please repeat that?

____ 4. Did I call at a bad time?

____ 5. Can I ask you a question?

____ 6. Is the boss going to quit?

____ 7. Was your son-in-law at home when you called?

a. No. He's going to retire.

b. Yes, you did.

c. Yes, he was.

d. No, it isn't.

e. No. I'm Italian.

f. Sure. What is it?

g. Sure. Walk three blocks to Main Street.

D. Same or Different?

Is the meaning the same or different?

1 "Nice to meet you."
"That's wonderful!"

    same (*different*)

2 "No, actually not."
"Not really."

    same   *different*

3 "That's too bad!"
"That's fantastic!"

    same   *different*

4 "Can you tell me how to get there?"
"Do you know how to get there?"

    same   *different*

5 "Where did you hear that?"
"I don't believe it!"

    same   *different*

6 "Excuse me."
"Pardon me."

    same   *different*

7 "I've got to go."
"I need to go."

    same   *different*

8 "Could you please repeat that?"
"Could you please say that again?"

    same   *different*

9 "Where are your things?"
"How are things?"

    same   *different*

10 "Are you with me so far?"
"Are you following me so far?"

    same   *different*

E. What's the Word?

Complete the sentences.

aren't	wasn't	weren't	don't	doesn't	didn't

1 My mother-in-law __didn't__ arrive yesterday.

2 Jennifer _____ want to move to another city.

3 The rush hour traffic _____ a problem last night. It was Saturday.

4 I'm sorry. We _____ have any rooms.

5 It's very cold today. The boys _____ going to go skiing.

6 We _____ very lucky yesterday. We got a speeding ticket.

F. The 5th Wheel!

Which one doesn't belong?

1 where   what   why   (wheel)   who

2 mother   brother   nephew   husband   father

3 Swedes   Koreans   Spaniards   Brazil   Japanese

4 pier   gate   track   platform   door

5 get a raise   win a prize   get fired   win the lottery   get a promotion

38

Describe Features of an Apartment

A. The Right Choice

Circle the correct word.

A.   (Where (How))**1** can I help you?

B.   We're looking for a two-bedroom (department   apartment)**2** near public transportation.

A.   Hmm. I think I have just what you're (looking for   looking at)**3**.

B.   Oh, good. (What   Where)**4** is it?

A.   It's on Porter Avenue.

B.   What kind of (neighbor   neighborhood)**5** is it?

A.   It's very (safe   safely)**6**.

B.   That sounds good. What can you (tell   say)**7** us about the apartment?

A.   Well, you'll love the kitchen! It has brand new (cabinets   stove)**8**!

B.   Hmm. Another question. (Do   Are)**9** cats allowed in the building?

A.   Cats? Yes, I believe they (do   are)**10**.

B.   How (large   much)**11** is the rent?

A. $850 a month.

B.   (Are   Does)**12** that include utilities?

A.   Everything except (electricity   utilities)**13**.

B. Matching Lines

Match the abbreviations and the words.

_c_	**1** conv.	a. electricity		___	**7** a/c	g. transportation
___	**2** mo.	b. including		___	**8** loc.	h. fireplace
___	**3** incl.	c. convenient		___	**9** utils.	i. air conditioning
___	**4** w/	d. building		___	**10** lge.	j. location
___	**5** bldg.	e. month		___	**11** fpl.	k. large
___	**6** elec.	f. with		___	**12** trans.	l. utilities

C. Listen

Listen and circle the word you hear.

1	(three-bedroom)	two-bedroom		**7**	driver	dryer
2	in town	downtown		**8**	included	including
3	$560	$650		**9**	near	close
4	electricity	utilities		**10**	talking	walking
5	beds	pets		**11**	neighborhood	neighbors
6	desire	quiet		**12**	rules	dues

D. Crosswalk

Across:
1. GARBAGE DISPOSAL
2. DISHWASHER
3. STOVE
4. (blank)
5. CABINETS
6. REFRIGERATOR

E. Matching Lines

Make associations.

c	**1**	waterbed	a.	kitchen	_	**7**	gas	g.	living room
d	**2**	one-bedroom	b.	location	_	**8**	fireplace	h.	neighborhood
_	**3**	dog	c.	bedroom	_	**9**	polite	i.	utilities
_	**4**	desirable	d.	apartment	_	**10**	6th floor	j.	rent
_	**5**	dishwasher	e.	transportation	j	**11**	$975	k.	neighbors
e	**6**	bus	f.	pet	_	**12**	safe	l.	building

A. Wrong Way!

Put the lines in the correct order.

_10_ Okay. Anything else besides the yogurt and the onions?

_7_ Four small containers. I guess we also need a few onions.

_4_ All right. What do you want me to get?

_9_ Let me think. How about three?

_1_ Could you do me a favor?

_11_ Yes. We're out of bread.

_5_ Well, could you pick up some yogurt?

_8_ How many should I get?

_2_ Certainly. What is it?

_13_ I think one loaf will be enough.

_3_ Could you run over to the store? We need a few things.

_6_ Some yogurt? Sure. How much?

_12_ Okay. How much bread do you want me to get?

_14_ Okay. So that's four small containers of yogurt, three onions, and a loaf of bread.

B. Listen

Listen and choose the correct response.

1
a. Let me think.
b. Sure. *(circled)*

2
a. Thanks a lot.
b. All right. *(circled)*

3
a. The store.
b. Some ground beef. *(circled)*

4
a. Okay. How much? *(circled)*
b. Okay. How many?

5
a. A small bunch. *(circled)*
b. A small head.

6
a. Half a pound. *(circled)*
b. Half a gallon.

7
a. Okay.
b. I think so. *(circled)*

8
a. A bottle.
b. A few cans. *(circled)*

9
a. Mineral water. *(circled)*
b. White bread.

10
a. Yes. A big stick.
b. Yes. A big tube. *(circled)*

11
a. A 4-ounce quart. *(circled)*
b. A 4-ounce jar.

12
a. Yes. A pint. *(circled)*
b. Yes. A pound.

C. Fill It In!

Fill in the correct answer.

1 We need _____ eggs.
    a. a pound of
    (b.) a dozen

2 Could you pick up _____ of milk?
    (a.) a quart
    b. a box

3 We need _____ of butter.
    a. two gallons
    (b.) two sticks

4 Please get _____ of orange juice.
    a. a tube
    (b.) a half gallon

5 We need _____ of peanut butter.
    (a.) a jar
    b. a bottle

6 Could you get _____ crackers?
    (a.) a box
    b. some

7 Could you pick up _____ lemons?
    (a.) three large
    b. a small jar of

8 Please get _____ of soda.
    a. half a dozen
    (b.) two six-packs

9 We need _____ of lettuce.
    a. a head
    (b.) a loaf

10 Let's get _____ of tuna fish.
    a. a box
    (b.) a few cans

11 Please pick up _____ avocados.
    a. a head of
    (b.) two or three

12 We also need _____ toothpaste.
    (a.) a small
    b. a tube

D. WordRap: *Shopping List*

Listen. Then clap and practice.

A. We need a loaf of bread.
B. Whole wheat or white?
A. I like whole wheat,
    But white's all right.

A. Could you pick up some apples
    And a bunch of grapes?
B. We also need cheese
    And some blank cassette tapes.

A. We're out of milk
    And ice cream, too.
B. Should I pick up some yogurt?
A. Yes. Please do!

A. We need some lettuce
    And a pound of rice.
B. How about some onions?
A. That would be nice!

A. Wrong Way!

Put the lines in the correct order.

__4__ No, "7."

__3__ I'm sorry. Did you say "Aisle 11"?

__6__ Any time.

__1__ Pardon me. Where can I find toothpicks?

__5__ Oh. Thanks a lot.

__2__ Toothpicks? They're in the Paper Products Section, Aisle 7.

B. What's the Line?

Complete the conversations.

1	2	3	4	5	6
Produce	Dairy	Frozen Food	Imported Foods	Paper Products	Household Supplies

1 A. Where can I find TV dinners?
B. _____ They're in the Frozen _____
_____ Food Section, Aisle 3. _____

2 A. Where can I find milk?
B. _It's in the Dairy_
Section. Aisle 2

3 A. Where can I find tortillas?
B. _They're in the I. Foods_
Section. Aisle 4

4 A. Where can I find ice cream?
B. _It's in the Frozen food_
Section. Aisle 3

5 A. Pardon me. Where's the lettuce?
B. _It's in the produce_
Section. Aisle 1

6 A. Where can I find toothpicks?
B. _They're in the Paper produds_
Section. Aisle 5

7 A. Excuse me. Where are the sponges?
B. _They'le in the household S._
Section. Aisle 6

8 A. Pardon me. Where's the cheese?
B. _It's in the Dairy_
Section. Aisle 2

C. Listen

Listen and choose the correct line to complete the conversation.

1 (a.) Yes. Aisle A.
    b. No. Aisle J.

4 a. Yes. Aisle B.
    b. Yes. Aisle C.

2 a. Yes. "G."
    b. No. "J."

5 a. No. "N."
    b. No. "M."

3 a. Yes. Aisle 9.
    b. No. Aisle 5.

6 a. Yes. Aisle 7.
    b. Yes. Aisle 11.

D. Mystery Products!

Unscramble each of these items. Where can you find them at the supermarket?

Dairy	Household Supplies	Paper Products
Frozen Food	Imported Foods	Produce

1 p n e s o g s   _sponges_   Look in the _Household Supplies_ Section.

2 a s t t m o o e   _tomatoes_   Look in the _products_ Section.

3 m k s i m k l i   _skim milk_   Look in the _Dairy_ Section.

4 p s i n k a n   _spainkn_   Look in the _Paper Product_ Section.

5 z o r f n e a p s e   _frozen pase_   Look in the _Frozen food_ Section.

6 o c t a h s s l e l   _taco ghells_   Look in the _Imported foods_ Section.

E. The 5th Wheel!

Which one doesn't belong?

1 (rice)   whole wheat bread   white bread   raisin bread

2 eggs   lemons   yogurt   Swiss cheese

3 sponges   napkins   toothpicks   peanut butter

4 chicken   onions   ground beef   lamb chops

5 check cashing   coffee   film developing   lottery tickets

6 tuna fish   avocados   peppers   potatoes

7 TV dinners   mayonnaise   ice cream   frozen yogurt

8 apples   butter   oranges   bananas

9 taco shells   tortillas   chili peppers   bug spray

10 toothpaste   cookies   cake   sugar

Evaluate the Cost of Food Items

Student Text Pages 66–67

A. Matching Lines

Which lines have the same meaning?

_c_ **1**   *That comes to a total of ten dollars.*

_e_ **2**   *That seems a little high to me.*

_b_ **3**   *How do you like that!*

_d_ **4**   *You can say THAT again!*

_a_ **5**   *Are you sure that's right?*

a. "I agree with you."

b. "I'm really surprised."

c. "That's the cost."

d. "Is that the correct amount?"

e. "I think that's expensive."

B. Matching Prices

Match the prices.

_e_ **1**	thirteen dollars and forty-five cents	a. $100.01
_K_ **2**	thirty-two dollars and twelve cents	b. $19.36
_b_ **3**	nineteen dollars and thirty-six cents	c. $8.79
_g_ **4**	twenty dollars and ten cents	d. $54.50
_i_ **5**	four dollars and sixty-one cents	e. $13.45
_h_ **6**	fifty-four dollars and fifteen cents	f. $10.23
_j_ **7**	seventeen dollars and sixteen cents	g. $20.10
_a_ **8**	one hundred dollars and one cent	h. $54.15
_d_ **9**	fifty-four dollars and fifty cents	i. $4.61
_c_ **10**	eight dollars and seventy-nine cents	j. $17.16
_f_ **11**	ten dollars and twenty-three cents	k. $32.12

45

C. Believable or Unbelievable?

Are the following prices "believable" or "unbelievable"?

		Believable	Unbelievable
1	"A jar of peanut butter is about $2.00."	✓	
2	"You can get a new car for $1,000.00."	✓	
3	"A newspaper costs about $10.00."		✓
4	"CDs are sometimes on sale for $10.99."	✓	
5	"Napkins cost about $1.50."	✓	
6	"You can get a pound of cheese for $3.00."	✓	
7	"A new house costs about $900.00."		✓
8	"A two-bedroom apartment costs $800.00 a month."	✓	
9	"A half gallon of milk costs about $.07."		✓
10	"You can get a dozen eggs for about $111.20."		✓

D. Listen

Listen and circle the correct price.

1	twelve fifteen	(twelve fifty)	6	thirteen thirty	(thirty thirteen)
2	ten forty-five	(ten fifty-four)	7	(one ninety-nine)	one eighty-nine
3	(two forty)	two fifty	8	nineteen cents	(ninety cents)
4	six sixty-seven	(six seventy-six)	9	three eighteen	(three eighty)
5	(twelve twenty-five)	twelve twenty	10	(one seventeen)	one seventy

E. Open Road!

Write a shopping list for yourself. What do you think each item will cost?

Item	Cost?

A. The Right Choice

Circle the correct words.

A. Mmm. ((These are) This is)[1] superb!
What (is it (are they))[2]?

B. (It's They're)[3] pancakes.

A. Pancakes?

B. Yes. (They're It's)[4] a popular American dish.

A. Well, (they're it's)[5] wonderful. What's in (it them)[6]?

B. Let me see . . . a (few little)[7] flour, a (few little)[8]
water, a (few little)[9] eggs, and . . . uh, oh yes, a
(few little)[10] milk.

A. (Are they Is it)[11] difficult to make?

B. No, not at all. I'll be happy to give you the recipe.

A. Mmm. (These are This is)[12] delicious!
What (is it are they)[13]?

B. (They're It's)[14] lasagna.

A. Lasagna?

B. Yes. (They're It's)[15] a popular Italian dish.

A. Well, (it's they're)[16] fantastic! What's in
(them it)[17]?

B. Let me see . . . a (few little)[18] ground beef, a
(little few)[19] tomato sauce, and a
(few little)[20] cheese.

A. (Is it Are they)[21] difficult to make?

B. No, not at all. I'll be happy to give you the recipe.

B. Open Road!

Tell about a new food you tried. What was it? What were the ingredients? Did you like it?

....

....

47

C. Listen

Do you remember the ingredients of the foods on student text page 68? Listen and write the number under the correct food.

borscht   *manicotti*   *enchiladas*   *moussaka*   *egg rolls*

   3   1   5   4   2

D. What's the Word?

Complete the conversations.

| it   them   sugar   ground beef   tomatoes   apples   chocolate   lettuce   eggs |

1
These hamburgers are superb! What's in __them__?

A little __ground beef__.

2
This salad is wonderful! What's in __it__?

Just a few __tomatoes__ and a little __lettuce__.

3
This apple cider is excellent! What's in __it__?

Just a few __apples__ and a little __shugar__

4
These cookies are great! What's in __it__?

A little __chocolate__ and a few __eggs__.

E. What's the Question?

Write the questions.

1 _____What are they_____?   They're tacos.

2 _____Wha is it_____?   It's a peanut butter sandwich.

3 __are they dificolt to make__?   No, not at all. They're easy to make.

4 _____what's in ct_____?   A few onions and a little sour cream.

Give Recipe Instructions

A. What's the Response?

Choose the correct response.

1 Your beef stew was fantastic!
  a. Yes. I'm with you.
  (b.) Oh, did you really like it?

2 Did you like it?
  (a.) Very much.
  b. Thank you very much.

3 It was superb!
  a. Could you repeat?
  (b.) Thank you for saying so.

4 Now I've got it. Is that it?
  (a.) That's it!
  b. I'll say!

5 Are you following me so far?
  a. Yes, I'm following with you.
  (b.) Yes, I'm with you.

6 Could I ask for the recipe?
  a. I'm sure.
  (b.) Sure.

7 Is it easy?
  (a.) It's really very easy.
  b. It's really excellent.

8 Thanks very much.
  a. You can say that again!
  (b.) My pleasure.

B. Sense or Nonsense?

Do the following "make sense" or are they "nonsense"?

		Sense	Nonsense
1	"Supermarkets sell vending machines."		✓
2	"Ice cream is in the Frozen Food Section."	✓	
3	"Butchers work in bakeries."		✓
4	"Money machines in supermarkets make money."		✓
5	"Some supermarkets have snack bars."	✓	
6	"Shampoo is in the Health Care Products Section."	✓	
7	"Some supermarkets are enormous."	✓	
8	"Fish markets sell screwdrivers and hammers."		✓
9	"You can buy ground beef at a butcher shop."	✓	
10	"Look for cheese in the Dairy Section."	✓	
11	"Specialty stores are for special people."		✓
12	"Neighborhood grocery stores are always larger than supermarkets."		✓

49

C. Fill It In!

Fill in the correct answer.

1 I need a bunch of _____.
    (a.) grapes
    b. mineral water

5 Don't forget to buy a head of _____.
    (a.) lettuce
    b. peanut butter

2 Please buy two tubes of _____.
    a. potato chips
    (b.) toothpaste

6 I need a pound of _____.
    a. cereal
    (b.) ground beef

3 We need a liter of _____.
    a. eggs
    (b.) apple juice

7 Please buy three cans of _____.
    (a.) baked beans
    b. mustard

4 Please get a few bags of _____.
    (a.) popcorn
    b. mayonnaise

8 Pick up a six-pack of _____.
    a. cinnamon
    (b.) soda

D. What's the Word?

Complete the recipe.

some	few	little	Cut up	Put	Add	Mix	Bake	Serve

Bob's Chicken Delight

____Cut up____ **1** ____Some____ **2** pieces of chicken,
a ____few____ **3** tomatoes, and ____few____ **4** onions.
____Put____ **5** the chicken, the tomatoes, and the onions
into a pan with a ____little____ **6** salt. ____Mix____ **7**
together a ____little____ **8** flour and ____some____ **9** water.
____at____ **10** a ____little____ **11** pepper to the flour and
water. ____put____ **12** the mixture into the pan with the
chicken, the tomatoes, the onions, and the salt.
____Kake____ **13** for two hours at 325 degrees.
____Seve____ **14** with a _____ **15** rolls
and a ____a litte____ **16** salad. Enjoy!

Exit 5

Tell About Work Skills

Student Text
Pages 76–77

A. What's the Word?

Complete the conversation.

we're	do	fill	I've	I'd	done	saw	sit	have

A. I _____saw_____ **1** your sign in the window.
    What position _____do_____ **2** you have open?

B. _____I've_____ **3** looking for a mechanic's assistant.

A. _____I'd_____ **4** like to apply.

B. _____ **5** you _____ **6** engine
    tune-ups before?

A. Yes, I _____have_____ **7**. _____ **8**
    _____ **9** engine tune-ups in my last two jobs.

B. Okay. Here's an application form. You can
    _____ **10** over there and _____ **11** it out.

A. Thank you.

B. Fill It In!

Fill in the correct answer.

1 I _____ in my present job.
   a. written advertisments
   (b.) write advertisments

2 _____ in my last two jobs.
   (a.) I've taken inventory
   b. I take inventory

3 I _____ in my last job.
   (a.) wrote obituaries
   b. write obituaries

4 I know how to _____.
   a. done tune-ups
   (b.) do tune-ups

5 _____ pizza in my present job.
   a. I'd made
   (b.) I make

6 _____ in my last three jobs.
   a. I've driven a bus
   (b.) I'd driven a bus

A. The Right Choice

Circle the correct word.

A. [Is / **Has**]¹ the manager [gone / go]² to the vault [already / yet]³?

B. Yes, she [**has** / is]⁴. [She's / She]⁵ [yet / already]⁶ [go / gone]⁷ there.

A. Oh, good. [What / When]⁸?

B. She [gone / went]⁹ there a little while ago.

A. [**Have** / Did]¹⁰ you [eat / **eaten**]¹¹ in the new cafeteria [yet / **already**]¹²?

B. Yes, I [have / do]¹³. [I've / You've]¹⁴ [already / yet]¹⁵ [eat / eaten]¹⁶ there.

A. [What / When]¹⁷?

B. I [ate / eaten]¹⁸ there at lunch time.

The food was great!

52

B. What's the Line?

Complete the conversations.

1 A. Has Carol given her presentation yet?
   B. Yes. __She's__ already __given__ it. __She gave__ it this morning.

2 A. Have the clerks gotten their raises yet?
   B. Yes. _____ already _____ them. _____ them yesterday.

3 A. Have you and Susan seen the report yet?
   B. Yes. __we'll__ already __seen__ it. __these__ it this morning.

4 A. Has David read his new contract yet?
   B. Yes. __he__ already __decided__ it. _____ it a little while ago.

5 A. Gloria, have you met the new supervisor yet?
   B. Yes. __I've__ already __met__ her. _____ her the other day.

C. Listen

Listen and circle the word you hear.

1 (wore)   worn   **4** spoke   spoken   **7** do   done

2 written   write   **5** meet   met   **8** seen see

3 made   make   **6** eaten   eat   **9** take taken

D. WordRap: *Work Talk!*

Listen. Then clap and practice.

A. Has he finished the report yet?
B. I don't know.
A. When did he start it?
B. An hour ago.

A. Has she gotten a raise?
B. It's hard to say.
    She wouldn't tell me,
    Anyway!

A. Have they moved their office?
    Are they still in the city?
B. They moved to the suburbs.
    It's very pretty.

A. Have you met the new boss?
    Does he seem okay?
B. He seems all right.
    But it's hard to say.

A. The Right Choice

Circle the correct word.

1 I've known how to use a computer (for (since)) 1990.

2 I've been interested in needlepoint (for   since) the last few years.

3 I've gotten a promotion every year (for   since) the past five years.

4 We've been English teachers at this school (for   since) last year.

5 I've eaten at the Ling Garden restaurant (for   since) many years.

B. Is or Has?

Check "is" or "has."

		is	*has*
1	He's known English for many years.		✓
2	He's traveling to Asia this summer.	✓	
3	She's learning to use a computer.		
4	It's been cold this winter.		
5	He's been interested in music since he was a child.		
6	There's an interesting museum near here.		
7	Where's he been?		
8	It's cold this winter.		
9	He's driven a truck since 1995.		
10	It's taken three hours to get home.		
11	She's already seen the newspaper today.		
12	She's happy to be on vacation.		
13	When's the concert?		
14	He's read the new contract.		
15	It's been a long hot summer!		
16	She's known my family for many years.		
17	There's a call for you on line 5.		
18	He's sung his last finale.		

C. Word Search

Find **8** past participles.

```
E R P I T A (S U N G) N B O D G S E B
T D L C A N A W A T L U P B U O A U
U O I Y K U I A N N R E A D N P T A
L N P R E P M A T T O R A T I C E E
Y E R E O P E H I P S F H K Z C N M
Q E T A U P S A I S C P T D B W N P
D G J S R L X N N W M T H O S P O R
K L D R H Y N G L X Z W M O N C B E
R S E E N A Z Y O U B I O Q A X N A
A X G S U G O N E S U B R E D S L A
O P I D S G O T T E N E E S B U E S
U B B A Y H I G H W C E T F R G S L
E A T T E N S U T D O N S A W A T J
```

D. Listen

These people are talking at a high school reunion. Listen and put a check next to the things they've done.

✔ He's written several books.

—— He's been a teacher.

—— He's been a counselor.

—— He's eaten unusual foods.

—— He's traveled to many places.

—— She's studied the banjo.

—— She's studied the piano.

—— She's given ballet lessons.

—— She's sung opera.

—— She's sung with a rock band.

E. Open Road!

How about you? What have YOU done in the past few years?

I've ....

I've ....

I've ....

A. Wrong Way!

Put the lines in the correct order.

___ Do you really think so?

_1_ Have you ever sold computers?

___ Oh, yes. I'm a hundred percent sure.

___ No, I haven't, but I've sold stereo equipment, and I'm confident I could learn to sell computers very easily.

B. Matching Lines

Match the questions and answers.

_e_ **1** Are you certain about that?   a. Yes, we have.

___ **2** Has your daughter ever taken ballet lessons?   b. Yes, he has.

___ **3** Have we ever gone to a nightclub?   c. No, she hasn't.

___ **4** Have you ever wanted to sell cars?   d. No, they haven't.

___ **5** Has your husband ever ridden a motorcycle?   e. I'm positive.

___ **6** Have your parents ever been to China?   f. Yes, you have.

___ **7** Have I asked too many questions?   g. No, I haven't.

C. Analogies

1 sing : sang *as* meet : ___met___   **5** went : gone *as* spoke : _____

2 write : written *as* eat : _____   **6** fly : flown *as* ride : _____

3 took : taken *as* drove : _____   **7** knew : known *as* got : _____

4 give : gave *as* do : _____   **8** wear : worn *as* read : _____

D. Listen

Listen and circle the word you hear.

1 have (has) haven't hasn't   **4** have has haven't hasn't

2 have has haven't hasn't   **5** have has haven't hasn't

3 have has haven't hasn't   **6** have has haven't hasn't

Discuss Job Performance

Student Text
Pages 84-85

A. The Right Choice

Circle the correct words.

A. Have you (repair   (repaired))[1] the van yet?

B. No, I (haven't   didn't)[2]. I was (thinking to   going to)[3] do it this afternoon.

A. Would you (peace   please)[4] do it as soon as possible? The van is supposed to be (repair   repaired)[5] by 2 o'clock.

B. I'm sorry. (I didn't known that   I didn't know that)[6]. I'll do it right away.

B. What's the Word?

Complete the sentences.

set	write	oil	polished	filled out	make	getting	fix
clean	typed	fed	arrange	vacuum	given out	spoken	eaten

1 Have you __given out__ the paychecks yet?

2 Have you _____ in the cafeteria yet?

3 Please _____ all the rugs in the office.

4 Are you __eaten__ the mail before lunch?

5 Have you _____ to your supervisor yet?

6 I _____ the tables in the lobby yesterday.

7 Have you __write__ your time sheet for this week?

8 Please _____ the conveyer belt before every shift.

9 Have you __set__ all the letters for Mr. Montenegro?

10 Will you please __make__ the flowers after your break?

11 The animals are supposed to be _____ at 11 o'clock sharp.

12 You're supposed to _____ the animal cages every morning.

13 We're planning to _____ the tables an hour before we open.

14 The Zorax Company is supposed to _____ the copy machine.

15 Can you please _____ all the beds the first thing in the morning?

16 I'd like you to _____ your monthly report by the last day of the month.

57

A. The Right Choice

Circle the correct words.

A. Are you able to sing and dance?

B. Yes. (We've been)¹ / We're — singing and dancing — for² / since — a long time.

A. For long³ / How long — ?

B. Since⁴ / For — we were teenagers.

A. Since you were teenagers⁵ / Since we were teenagers — ?

B. Yes, that's right⁶ / that right — .

A. Well, you certainly have a lot of experience.

B. I guess we do.

B. Listen

Which sentence do you hear?

1 ⓐ a. I've been using the Internet since 1995.
    b. I've been doing the Internet since 1995.

4 a. He's been repairing them for more than five years.
    b. He's been preparing them for more than five years.

2 a. I've been baking for years.
    b. I've been breaking them for years.

5 a. They've been living there for a year.
    b. They've been leaving there for a year.

3 a. She's been cleaning the animals.
    b. She's been feeding the animals.

6 a. You've been walking for an hour.
    b. You've been talking for an hour.

C. What's the Line?

Complete the conversations.

1 A. Do they make copies in Shipping?
    B. Yes. <u>They've been making</u> copies for two months.

2 A. Is Rita writing her monthly report?
    B. Yes. _____ it for the past two hours.

3 A. Can you operate a conveyor belt?
    B. Yes. _____ one since I started working here.

4 A. Can you and your brother repair cars?
    B. Yes. _____ them since we were teenagers.

5 A. Is Frank still fixing the copy machine?
    B. Yes. _____ it since 7:30 this morning.

6 A. Can you cook and bake?
    B. Yes. _____ since I moved away from home.

D. Open Road!

Tell about yourself.

I've been living in .... (for since) ....

I've been studying English at .... (for since) ....

I've been working at .... (for since) ....

I've been .... (for since) ....

I've been .... (for since) ....

A. Wrong Way!

Put the lines in the correct order.

____ Certainly. What would you like to know?

____ Well, the zookeeper's primary responsibility is to oversee the employees and the animals.

____ Definitely! In my present job, I've been overseeing the animals and employees for years. And I wrote advertisements in the job I had before that.

_1_ Can you tell me anything more about the position?

____ In addition, the zookeeper writes advertisements for the zoo. Do you think you could handle those responsibilities?

____ I see.

____ What exactly are the zookeeper's responsibilities?

B. Listen

Listen to each person's work history, and put a check next to the correct information.

1
- ✔ He's been doing tune-ups.
- ____ He changes tires.
- ✔ He changed tires before.

2
- ____ She's been selling furniture.
- ____ She sells refrigerators.
- ____ She sold dishwashers before.

3
- ____ He's been writing news stories.
- ____ He writes obituaries.
- ____ He wrote news stories before.

4
- ____ She's been taking inventory.
- ____ She's been driving the van.
- ____ She drove the van before.

C. Open Road!

What responsibilities have you had in your jobs?

1 In my present job, I've been ....

2 In the job I had before that, I ....

A. Good Advice or Bad Advice?

Decide if each of the following is good advice or bad advice for someone going to a job interview.

		Good Advice	Bad Advice
1	"Dress cleanly and neatly."	✓	
2	"Bring a copy of your resume."		
3	"Don't shake hands with the employer."		
4	"Be punctual."		
5	"Don't be polite."		
6	"Wait for the employer to invite you to sit down."		
7	"Don't look directly into the eyes of the interviewer."		
8	"Chew gum during the interview."		
9	"Don't prepare a list of questions about the job."		
10	"Be ready to answer questions about previous jobs."		
11	"Don't answer difficult questions."		
12	"Talk confidently about previous work experience."		
13	"Don't be truthful about your skills and abilities."		
14	"Say thank you for the time the person has spent with you."		

B. Listen

Listen to the interviews. What did each job applicant do wrong?

1.
   a. Mr. Smally didn't dress appropriately for the interview.
   b. Mr. Smally wasn't prepared to answer questions about his previous work experience.
   c. Mr. Smally didn't smile at the interviewer.

2.
   a. Ms. Short wasn't honest.
   b. Ms. Short wasn't capable and well-prepared.
   c. Ms. Short wasn't punctual.

3.
   a. Mr. Curtis didn't bring his resume to the interview.
   b. Mr. Curtis brought his family to the interview.
   c. Mr. Curtis wasn't honest with the interviewer.

4.
   a. Ms. Jackson wasn't on time.
   b. Ms. Jackson wasn't confident and truthful.
   c. Ms. Jackson asked inappropriate questions.

C. What's the Question?

What are the interviewer's questions?

1 A. _____ Where have you worked before _____?

B. I've worked at the Spandex Company and the Ajax Corporation.

2 A. How long have do you work in Ajax Corporation?

B. I worked at the Ajax Corporation from 1990 to 1995.

3 A. What is your responsabilities in your Job?

B. My responsibilities? I typed reports and did the payroll.

4 A. do you work now?

B. No, I don't work now. I'm a student.

5 A. How long you studing?

B. I've been a student since last September.

6 A. what have you been studying?

B. I've been studying accounting and finance.

7 A. Wen will you finis tha school?

B. I'll finish school next month.

8 A. do you have any questions?

B. Yes. I have some questions about the company.

D. Fill It In!

Fill in the correct answer.

1 Job interviews are ____.
    (a.) critical
    b. capable

2 I have a very important ____.
    a. resume
    (b.) position

3 What ____ do you do in your job?
    (a.) exactly
    b. certainly

4 It's important to make a good ____.
    a. interview
    (b.) impression

5 Many ____ apply for the same position.
    (a.) applicants
    b. employers

6 My son has a new job with a lot of ____.
    a. experience
    (b.) responsibilities

Report an Emergency

A. Matching Lines

Match the lines.

_d_	**1**	My father has just fallen down a flight of stairs.
_a_	**2**	Someone has just broken into my house.
_e_	**3**	A fire has just broken out in my house.
_b_	**4**	My hot water heater has just flooded my basement.
_c_	**5**	A squirrel has just crawled into my house through the chimney.

a. We'll send a squad car right away.

b. We'll send a repairperson right away.

c. We'll send an animal removal specialist right away.

d. We'll send an ambulance right away.

e. We'll send an engine unit right away.

B. Listen

Listen and choose the next line of the conversation.

1
　a. Could you send a repairperson right now?
　b. Could you send a medical specialist right away?

2
　a. Call the carpenter!
　b. Call the ambulance service!

3
　a. Call the fire department!
　b. Call the electrician!

4
　a. Can you send an animal removal team right now?
　b. Can you send a police squad car right away?

5
　a. Call the ASPCA right now!
　b. Call the heating company right now!

6
　a. Call the police emergency unit!
　b. Call the ASPCA right away!

C. Open Road!

Report an emergency. What do you say?

A. _911_

B. There's been an emergency!

A. _____

B. _____

A. _____

A. The Right Choice

Circle the correct word.

A. Police.

B. I want to ((report) tell)[1] an accident.

A. Yes. (Get   Go)[2] ahead.

B. A truck has (overtuned   overturned).[3]

A. What's your name?

B. Marilyn Jones.

A. (When   Where)[4] did the accident (overturned   happen)[5]?

B. (At   On)[6] the expressway (near   close)[7] Exit 45.

A. Did you (say   tell)[8] Exit 49?

B. No, Exit 45.

A. All (okay   right).[9] We'll (is   be)[10] there right away.

B. What's the Word?

Complete each sentence with the correct form of the verb.

run over	fall through	break out	break into	fall down
rob	overturn	mug	land	crawl

1. Two people have just ____robbed____ a jewelry store on Main Street!

2. A helicopter has just _____ in the mall parking lot!

3. My grandmother has _____ the stairs!

4. Someone has just _____ my apartment!

5. A large truck has just _____ on the expressway!

6. A fire has _____ in my neighbor's house!

7. A skunk has _____ into my basement through a window!

8. An elderly couple has been _____ in front of the church!

9. Two children have been _____ by a car at 1600 Riverside Avenue!

10. Two workmen have _____ the roof of a house on Madison Avenue!

A. What's the Response?

Choose the correct response.

1. Can you recommend something for a bad headache?

   a. I'd recommend nasal spray.
   b. I'd recommend aspirin tablets.

2. Can you suggest something for frizzy hair?

   a. Try hair spray.
   b. Try skin lotion.

3. What do you recommend for a stuffy nose?

   a. I suggest nasal spray.
   b. I suggest a cold.

4. Can you suggest something for dry skin?

   a. I'd suggest dry weather.
   b. I suggest dry skin lotion.

5. Can you recommend something for itchy, watery eyes?

   a. Try eyedrops.
   b. Try cold tablets.

6. What do you recommend for a bad backache?

   a. I'd suggest rest.
   b. I'd suggest freezing weather.

B. Listen

Listen and choose the correct answer.

1. a. This person has a cold.
   b. This person has an earache.

2. a. This person is at home.
   b. This person is in a drug store.

3. a. The medicine is in Aisle D.
   b. The medicine is in Aisle C.

4. a. This person has a bad cold.
   b. This person has a backache.

5. a. Eyedrops are on the middle shelf.
   b. Eyedrops are on the bottom shelf.

6. a. This medicine is on the first shelf.
   b. This medicine is on the third shelf.

7. a. This person is looking for eyedrops.
   b. This person has a headache.

8. a. Hair spray is in the back of the store.
   b. Hair spray is in the front of the store.

65

Describe Symptoms and Make a Doctor's Appointment

A. What's the Response?

Choose the correct response.

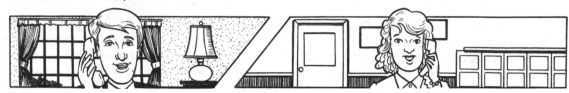

1 Hello. This is Paul Perkins calling.
    a. Doctor's office.
    (b.) What can I do for you?

2 I'm not feeling very well.
    a. What am I feeling?
    (b.) What's the problem?

3 What seems to be wrong?
    (a.) I feel dizzy and nauseous.
    b. I think I'm right.

4 I can't move my arm.
    (a.) I see.
    b. I'm sure.

5 How long have you been dizzy?
    a. Since three days.
    (b.) For three days.

6 Would you like to make an appointment?
    a. I want to make an appointment.
    (b.) Yes, please.

7 Is 3:00 tomorrow afternoon convenient?
    a. 3:00 tomorrow afternoon?
    b. Are you sure?

8 That's fine. Thank you very much.
    a. Okay. See you tomorrow.
    b. I haven't been feeling very well.

B. What's the Word?

Complete the sentences.

aren't	haven't	has	since
isn't	hasn't	had	for

1 My dog ___has___ been refusing to eat ___for___ three days.

2 My husband ___has___ had a terrible toothache for the past week.

3 I'm sorry you ___aren't___ feeling well.

4 The doctor ___isn't___ in the office now.

5 I've ___had___ a migraine headache all day.

6 Everyone at work ___has___ been dizzy and nauseous today.

7 My friend's ear ___has___ been ringing ___since___ Saturday.

8 The students in my English class ___haven't___ been feeling well this week.

9 My cat Chester is sick. He ___hasn't___ eaten his cat food _____ a week.

66

C. Crosswalk

headache	toothache	dizzy	nauseous	backache
sore throat	stuffy nose	cough	watery eyes	dry skin

D. Listen

Listen and choose the sentence to finish the conversation.

1
  a. Call the dentist right away.
  (b.) Call the doctor's office right away.

2
  (a.) Call the animal hospital.
  b. Why don't you call the pharmacist?

3
  (a.) I suggest you tell the supervisor.
  b. I suggest you call the dentist.

4
  (a.) Call the dentist right away.
  b. Call an ambulance right away.

5
  a. Call the animal hospital.
  (b.) Call an eye and ear doctor.

6
  (a.) Ask a pharmacist for some lotion.
  b. Ask a pharmacist for some tablets.

7
  a. Call the emergency medical team.
  (b.) Call the animal hospital.

8
  a. He needs to see an ambulance.
  (b.) He needs to see a doctor.

9
  (a.) Let's call the highway patrol.
  b. Let's call a mechanic.

10
  a. Call the heating company.
  (b.) Call the emergency medical team.

Ask About and Give a Medical History

A. The Right Choice

Circle the correct words.

A. Well, Ms. Kramer, I think you've **giving / (given)** [1] me almost all the information I need for

your medical history. Just one or two more **medical histories / questions** [2] , if that's okay.

B. **Confidently / Certainly** [3] .

A. Do you **had / have** [4] back trouble?

B. No, I **don't / haven't** [5] .

A. And have you **ever / never** [6] **have / had** [7] a bad

reaction to any drugs?

B. No, I **didn't / haven't** [8] .

A. All right, Ms. Kramer. Please take a seat.

The doctor will **been / be** [9] with you in a few minutes.

68

B. What's the Question?

Write the questions.

1 A. _____ Has your husband ever been hospitalized _____?
   B. No, my husband has never been hospitalized.

2 A. _____?
   B. Yes, I'm allergic to penicillin.

3 A. _____?
   B. No, my dog Rover has never been on a special diet.

4 A. _____?
   B. No, my mother doesn't have any objection to herbs or other natural remedies.

5 A. _____?
   B. No, I don't have any history of heart disease in my family.

6 A. _____?
   B. No, my daughter has never had surgery before.

7 A. _____?
   B. No, I've never had a toothache before.

8 A. _____?
   B. Okay. I'll answer one or two more questions.

C. Sense or Nonsense?

Do the following "make sense" or are they "nonsense"?

		Sense	*Nonsense*
1	"Doctors use many different remedies for diseases."	✓	_____
2	"I'm allergic to stuffy noses."	_____	_____
3	"Mr. Fenn is in back trouble."	_____	_____
4	"I'm allergic to several medicines."	_____	_____
5	"What diseases do you take?"	_____	_____
6	"We're going to make your medical history."	_____	_____
7	"I'm on a special diet."	_____	_____
8	"My wife has been hospitalized three times."	_____	_____
9	"The doctor will take your seat in a few minutes."	_____	_____

A. The Right Choice

Choose the correct answer.

1 I'm concerned about your blood pressure.
    (a.) I urge you to change your diet.
    b. I urge you to stop going to rock concerts.

Do you have any suggestions that might help?
    c. You should eat more salty food.
    (d.) You should look for a cookbook that has low-fat recipes.

2 I'm concerned about your back.
    a. I urge you to join an organization to help you "kick the habit."
    b. I strongly advise you to begin a daily exercise routine.

Do you have any suggestions that might help?
    c. You might join a yogurt class.
    d. You should do sit-ups every day.

3 I'm concerned about your hearing.
    a. I strongly advise you to change your eating habits.
    b. I urge you to change your music listening habits.

Do you have any suggestions that might help?
    c. You might stop going to rock concerts.
    d. You should start going to rock concerts.

B. Listen

Listen and choose the sentence that is closest in meaning.

1
    a. You've joined an organization to help you "kick the habit."
    (b.) You ought to join an organization to help you "kick the habit."

2
    a. You have to cut back on your responsibilities.
    b. Your back is your responsibility.

3
    a. You might change your eating habits.
    b. You need to change your eating habits.

4
    a. I think you could find a hobby that you enjoy.
    b. You might have a good idea about that hobby.

5
    a. It's necessary for you to begin an exercise routine.
    b. You've had an exercise routine.

6
    a. You might eat less salty food.
    b. You must eat less salty food.

A. Wrong Way!

Put the lines in the correct order.

____ I understand. Two pills after each meal.

____ Oh?

____ I see. Well, thanks very much.

_1_ Okay. Here's your prescription.

____ That's right. And one more thing. You could possibly feel dizzy after taking this medication.

____ Now be sure to follow the directions on the label. You need to take two pills after each meal.

____ Yes, but don't worry. That's a common side effect.

____ Thank you.

B. The 5th Wheel!

Which one doesn't belong?

1	You're supposed to	(You could possibly)	You've got to	You must
2	You may	It's possible that	You need to	You could possibly
3	It's essential	You could	You have to	You must
4	I suggest	Why don't you?	You have to	I'd recommend
5	You could	I urge you to	You might	It might be a good idea
6	What's the matter?	Can you suggest?	What's wrong?	What's the problem?
7	What was that?	What did you say?	What's that?	Can you recommend?

C. Listen

Listen and circle the word you hear.

1	(they)	they're	**3**	they're	their	**5**	they'll	they're
2	they'll	they've	**4**	their	they're	**6**	they'll	they've

71

D. What's the Ailment?

Read the solutions to common medical problems from student text page 108 and figure out the ailment.

sore throat	stomachache	cold	nose bleed	bee sting

1 "Pinch your nose."   nose bleed

2 "Drink warm milk with honey, or lemon juice and honey."   _____

3 "Take some antacids."   _____

4 "Put a little vinegar on the skin."   _____

5 "Have a bowl of homemade chicken soup."   _____

6 "Drink some peppermint tea."   _____

7 "Gargle with warm salty water."   _____

8 "Tilt your head backward and rest it on the back of a chair."   _____

E. WordRap: *My Doctor's Advice*

Listen. Then clap and practice.

You've got to be careful
What you eat.
Cut out sugar!
Cut down on meat!

Give up this!
Give up that!
Exercise!
And you won't get fat!

Take this medicine.
Do it right!
Take one in the morning
And two at night.

Read the directions
Carefully.
Take one at nine
And one at three.

F. Open Road!

Tell about your favorite home remedy.

....

....

Offer Someone Medical Advice

A. Wrong Way!

Put the lines in the correct order.

____ Sure. What?

____ I have a bloody nose!

____ What's the problem?

_1_ Oh, no!

____ You ought to pinch your nose.

____ Well . . . You might tilt your head backward and
rest it on the back of a chair.

____ Oh, that's too bad. Can I offer a suggestion?

____ Hmm. I'll give it a try. Thanks.

____ You know, I've tried pinching my nose when I've had a bloody
nose before, and that doesn't work for me. Any other suggestions?

B. What's the Problem?

Decide what each person's problem is.

 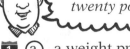

1 (a.) a weight problem
b. a hair problem

2 a. a stomachache
b. a sore shoulder

3 a. a fever
b. the hiccups

 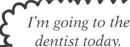

4 a. a backache
b. an earache

5 a. a toothache
b. a headache

6 a. allergies
b. remedies

7 a. a cold
b. an earache

8 a. a toothache
b. the flu

9 a. the hiccups
b. heart disease

73

A. The Right Choice

Circle the correct words.

1 We need [a little / (a few)] potatoes.

2 How [many / much] is the rent?

3 Please pick up [a / some] avocados.

4 Add [a little / a few] tomatoes to the stew.

5 Please get [a / some] six-pack of soda.

6 Try to get [a gallon / a pound] of chicken.

7 How [much / many] apples do you want?

8 Please buy [a head / a bunch] of cabbage.

B. Matching Lines

Match the lines.

_e_ **1** You have to take these pills.

___ **2** I advise you to change your diet.

___ **3** You must stop smoking.

___ **4** A truck has just overturned on the expressway.

___ **5** I know a good home remedy for a cold.

___ **6** Mary has a terrible migraine headache.

___ **7** Look at your hair! It's frizzy!

___ **8** A fire just broke out on Park Street!

___ **9** I haven't had my job interview yet.

___ **10** He's supposed to start exercising.

a. When are you going to have it?

b. It must be the humidity.

c. She should call her doctor.

d. Drink hot water with lemon and honey.

e. Take them three times a day before meals.

f. The highway patrol will be there right away.

g. You ought to eat less salty food.

h. He has to do sit-ups every day.

i. Call the fire department.

j. I'm concerned about your lungs.

C. Fill It In!

Fill in the correct answer.

1 _____ a delivery van.
  (a.) I've driven
  b. I'd driven

2 Has he _____ his promotion yet?
  a. got
  b. gotten

3 _____ in this building for a year.
  a. He's been leaving
  b. He's been living

4 I've already _____ the paychecks.
  a. given out
  b. gave out

5 _____ news stories every day.
  a. We've wrote
  b. We write

6 How long has she _____ type?
  a. is able to
  b. been able to

7 What _____ your responsibilities?
  a. are
  b. have

8 I haven't seen you _____ July.
  a. for
  b. since

9 It's _____ since Saturday.
  a. raining
  b. been raining

10 How long have you _____ them?
  a. known
  b. knew

11 Have you _____ used a computer?
  a. ever
  b. never

12 _____ have you been here?
  a. How long
  b. So long

13 _____ difficult to make?
  a. Have been
  b. Are they

14 _____ moussaka.
  a. I've never eaten
  b. I never eaten

15 _____ exercise next week.
  a. They'll
  b. They'd

16 _____ allergic to cats before.
  a. She's ever been
  b. She's never been

D. Listen

Listen and choose the best response.

1 a. I wasn't aware of that.
  (b.) Sure. I'd be happy to.
  c. Thanks a lot.

2 a. Can you sell computers?
  b. Now I've got it.
  c. Are you certain about that?

3 a. I'll say!
  b. What's new with you?
  c. You're supposed to.

4 a. You could make manicotti.
  b. I'm positive about that.
  c. Why don't you make pizza?

5 a. I'm sorry. I didn't realize that.
  b. I'm sure.
  c. Let me think.

6 a. You're welcome.
  b. Yes. I'm positive.
  c. Can I ask you a question?

7 a. That's too bad.
  b. I recommend that.
  c. That's right.

8 a. What's happening?
  b. You might try yoga.
  c. Who told you that?

Exit 7

Locate Items in a Department Store

Student Text
Pages
116-117

A. Wrong Way!

Put the lines in the correct order.

____ Certainly. Take the escalator down two floors.

____ Stereos? They're in the Home Entertainment Department on the ground level.

____ Thank you very much.

_1_ Pardon me. Where are stereos located?

____ On the ground level? I see. Can you tell me how to get there?

B. Matching Lines

Match the items and departments.

_e_ **1** beds

____ **2** microwave ovens

____ **3** pots and pans

____ **4** kids' jeans

____ **5** neckties

____ **6** dresses

____ **7** CD players

____ **8** returns

Directory

a. Children's Clothing

b. Women's Clothing

c. Customer Service

d. Home Entertainment

e. Furniture

f. Housewares

g. Men's Clothing

h. Household Appliances

C. Listen

Listen and put a check next to the sentence you hear.

1 ✔ Dishwashers are on "9."

____ Dishwashers are fine.

2 ____ Returns are near the rear door.

____ Returns are at the rear of the store.

3 ____ Gloves are near the right entrance.

____ Gloves are near the side entrance.

4 ____ Women's shoes are in Aisle G.

____ Women's shoes are in Aisle 3.

D. What Am I?

Which department store item is "speaking"?

headphones	pastry	dishes	necktie	videocassette recorder
stove	television	coat	shoes	designer dress

1 "I'll be very important to you when you go outside next winter." _____coat_____

2 "If you rent a movie, I'll play it." _____

3 "You wear me on your feet every day." _____

4 "Come to the snack bar and enjoy me!" _____

5 "I'll cook dinner for you tonight." _____

6 "Mr. Miller will need me for his job interview." _____

7 "Turn me on and watch your favorite programs!" _____

8 "I hope you wash me after every meal!" _____

9 "Wear me to a friend's wedding!" _____

10 "If you don't want to have hearing problems, you should cut down on my use." _____

E. Fill It In!

Fill in the correct answer.

1 Dinner dishes are in the ____.
   a. side door
   (b.) basement

2 Where can I find ____?
   a. kitchen sets
   b. floors

3 Can you tell me ____?
   a. how to get there
   b. the first level

4 You can find lamps ____.
   a. in the side door
   b. near the side door

5 Women's blouses are on the ____.
   a. fourth floor
   b. rear

6 Go to ____ to return that.
   a. Custom Service
   b. Customer Service

7 ____ the escalator over there.
   a. Make
   b. Take

8 Could you tell me ____ the elevator is?
   a. where
   b. how

9 Walk up this staircase one ____.
   a. building
   b. flight

10 The elevator is on the ____.
   a. right in the corner
   b. corner in the right

11 Stereos? They're near the ____.
   a. floor
   b. rear door

12 Where are the TVs ____?
   a. located
   b. locate

Select Items in a Department Store

A. The Right Choice

Circle the correct words.

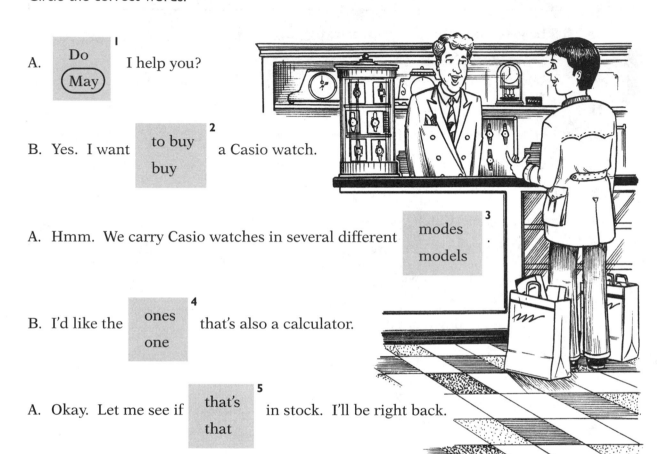

A. | Do
(May) |¹ I help you?

B. Yes. I want | to buy
buy |² a Casio watch.

A. Hmm. We carry Casio watches in several different | modes
models |³ .

B. I'd like the | ones
one |⁴ that's also a calculator.

A. Okay. Let me see if | that's
that |⁵ in stock. I'll be right back.

B. Sense or Nonsense?

Do the following "make sense" or are they "nonsense"?

		Sense	*Nonsense*
1	"This ice maker has a 19-inch screen."	_____	✓
2	"This computer has 8 megabytes of memory."	_____	_____
3	"I bought a vacuum cleaner that's also a calculator."	_____	_____
4	"This color TV has a 13-inch screen and a remote control."	_____	_____
5	"This refrigerator has a self-cleaning oven."	_____	_____
6	"This microwave beeps when the food is ready."	_____	_____
7	"You should definitely get the waterproof coffeemaker."	_____	_____
8	"I recommend that you buy a refrigerator with remote control."	_____	_____

C. Listen

Listen and circle the product the customer wants to buy.

1. (gas range)   TV
2. watch   refrigerator
3. coffeemaker   computer
4. computer   TV
5. coffeemaker   gas range
6. watch   refrigerator

D. Crosswalk

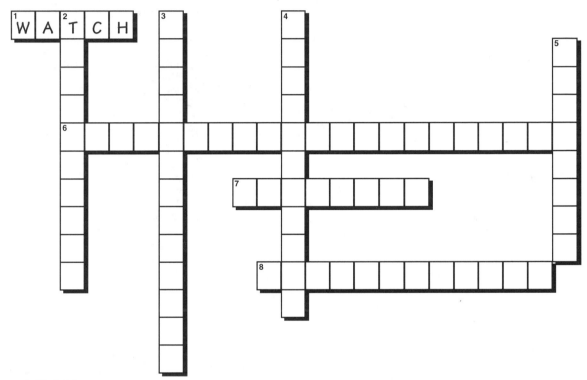

ACROSS

1. Is this one waterproof?
6. They're interested in one with remote control.
7. Does he have a personal one at home?
8. I want one with an automatic ice maker.

DOWN

2. Let me look at the one with a 27-inch screen.
3. This one beeps when the food is ready.
4. I need one that makes 12 cups.
5. We want one with a self-cleaning oven.

E. Open Road!

Recommend a product to a friend.

When you buy a ...., you should buy one with

....

Purchase Items in a Department Store

A. The Right Choice

Circle the correct words.

A. Pardon me. (When (Could))[1] you help me?

B. (I'd be   I've be)[2] happy to. What can
I (make   do)[3] for you?

A. I'm looking for a (press   sleeveless)[4] blouse
for my (son   daughter)[5].

B. (What   Whose)[6] size does she wear?

A. Size medium . . . (I'm thinking   I think)[7].

B. What color (could   would)[8] you like?

A. Bright purple, if (you've had   you have)[9] it.

B. Okay. Let's see . . . a size medium bright purple
sleeveless blouse. Do you think your daughter will
like this (ones   one)[10]?

A. Yes. I'm sure she will. (I'd take   I'll take)[11] it.

B. Will this be cash or charge?

A. Do you (take   make)[12] VISA?

B. No. I'm afraid not. We only accept our own store
credit (cash   card)[13].

A. Oh. In that case, I'll pay (credit card   cash)[14].

B. Matching Lines

Match the description and the item.

_e_   **1** I'd like size 7 black ____.   a. TV

____   **2** I'm looking for a permanent press dress ____.   b. coffeemaker

____   **3** Do you have a 25-inch color ____?   c. belt

____   **4** I'm looking for a size 38 brown leather ____.   d. blouse

____   **5** I'd like a small light green sleeveless ____.   e. sneakers

____   **6** Do you have a beige 8-cup ____?   f. watch

____   **7** I'm looking for a waterproof ____.   g. shirt

C. Wrong Way!

Put the words in the correct order.

1 a jogging red, white, and blue suit   <u>a red, white, and blue jogging suit</u>

2 a self-cleaning range gas   _____

3 an machine washing automatic   _____

4 jeans designer light blue   _____

5 a waterproof brown dark watch   _____

6 size 7 sneakers white   _____

7 a shirt light blue press permanent   _____

8 a leather large belt   _____

9 an Computer Personal IBM   _____

10 a yellow small purse plastic   _____

11 permanent press beige pants   _____

12 a dark green sleeveless medium blouse   _____

D. Listen

Listen and choose the best response.

1 a. How large is the screen?
   b. Is it a black-and-white TV?

2 a. Is it for your living room?
   b. Where did you get it?

3 a. Do they have a V-neck?
   b. Are they designer jeans?

4 a. Is it a size 36?
   b. Is it leather or plastic?

5 a. I recommend one with a manual transmission.
   b. I recommend one with no transmission.

6 a. What size do you wear?
   b. What color does he like?

7 a. You should buy a 12-cup one.
   b. You should buy a leather one.

8 a. Is it automatic?
   b. Does it have a V-neck?

9 a. General Electric makes good ranges.
   b. Do you want one that beeps?

10 a. You should definitely get one with leather belts.
   b. You should get one with leather upholstery.

A. The Right Choice

Circle the correct words.

A. (I'd want to (I want to))[1] return these earrings.

B. All right. Do you have the (recipe (receipt))[2]?

A. Yes. Here you are.

B. (Would (Could))[3] I ask why you're returning
((them) it)[4]?

A. Yes. ((Their) They're)[5] (to (too))[6] large.

B. Would you like to (rechange (exchange))[7]
(it (them))[8] for smaller ((ones) one)[9]?

A. No, I don't think so. (I (I'd))[10] just like a
((refund) return)[11], please.

B. Certainly.

B. What's the Word?

1	*jeans:*	difficult	powerful	(tight)	young
2	*sofa:*	easy	comfortable	V-neck	automatic
3	*shirt:*	permanent press	plastic	8-cup	easy
4	*merchandise:*	powerful	in stock	tall	automatic
5	*prices:*	lightweight	sleeveless	bright	low
6	*VCR:*	expensive	conservative	tight	tall

C. WordRap: *Shopping Problems!*

Listen. Then clap and practice.

This suit doesn't fit.
Everything's wrong!
The sleeves are too short,
And the pants are too long!
It's not my size.
The jacket's too tight!
It's not my style,
And the color's not right!

These shoes are too small!
They look like a seven.
They aren't my size.
I need an eleven!
These gloves are too short,
And the color's all wrong!
I need a large size.
My fingers are long!

D. What's the Word?

Complete the following with the correct form of the adjective.

lightweight	fancy	big	short
powerful	easy	cheap	tight

1. This walkie-talkie set is too weak. I want one that's ___more powerful___.

2. These pajamas are too long. I need a ___short___ pair.

3. This briefcase is too heavy. I want one that's ___lightweight___.

4. These jeans are too large. I'd like to try a ___tight___ pair.

5. I'd like to exchange this dress for one that's ___fancy___. This one is too conservative.

6. I'd like to exchange these shoes for ones that are ___cheap___. These are too expensive.

7. This computer game is too difficult. I want one that's ___easyer___.

8. This vest is too small. I'd like to try a ___bigger___ one.

E. Listen

Listen and choose the best response.

1.
a. Those are more lightweight.
b. The ones over there are lighter. *(circled)*

2.
a. That one is simpler. *(circled)*
b. That one is more powerful.

3.
a. I'll try to find a darker one.
b. I'll try to find a fancier one. *(circled)*

4.
a. Let's look for a lighter one.
b. Let's look for a smaller one. *(circled)*

5.
a. I'm sure we can find a larger one. *(circled)*
b. I'm sure we can find a tighter one.

6.
a. Let's look for a shorter one.
b. Let's look for a more powerful one. *(circled)*

7.
a. Certainly. Is this one too long? *(circled)*
b. Certainly. Is this one too tall?

8.
a. The prices at Value World are lower. *(circled)*
b. The prices at Value World are simpler.

83

Access the Services of a Post Office

A. Fill It In!

Fill in the correct answer.

1 I'd like to ____ this package.
   a. apply for
   (b.) mail

2 Sorry. You've got the ____ window.
   (a.) wrong
   b. right

3 I'd like to ____ a registered letter.
   (a.) send
   b. buy

4 Yes, you're at the ____ window.
   a. wrong
   (b.) right

5 Money orders can be ____ at the next window.
   (a.) purchased
   b. filed

6 Your mail is at the ____.
   a. box
   b. post office

7 I want to apply for ____.
   (a.) some packages
   b. a post office box

8 Stamps can be ____ at Window 2.
   (a.) bought
   b. mailed

9 I'd like to purchase a ____.
   a. change of address form
   (b.) money order

10 Aerogrammes can be ____ at Window 3.
   (a.) gotten
   b. got

B. Listen

Listen and choose the correct answer.

Conversation 1

Conversation 2

1 a. The package is going to Boston.
   (b.) The package is going to Houston.

2 a. The package weighs seven pounds.
   b. The package weighs eleven pounds.

3 a. First class is $8.75.
   b. Parcel post is $8.75.

4 a. The customer decides to send the package parcel post.
   b. The customer decides to send the package first class.

5 a. The package is going to Miami.
   b. The package is going to Naomi.

6 a. It's cheaper to send it parcel post.
   b. It's cheaper to send it first class.

7 a. Parcel post is faster.
   b. First class is faster.

8 a. The customer decides to send the package parcel post.
   b. The customer decides to send the package first class.

C. Matching Lines

Match the questions and answers.

_d_ **1** How would you like to send this package?

_f_ **2** How much does it weigh?

_a_ **3** Eighteen dollars and forty cents?

_c_ **4** How much do I owe you?

_g_ **5** Will it take longer by parcel post?

_b_ **6** When do you need it to get there?

_e_ **7** Is it cheaper to send it parcel post?

a. Yes. That's what it'll cost to send it first class.

b. It has to be there by this Friday.

c. Eighteen dollars and forty cents.

d. First class, please.

e. Yes. It'll take ten days to get there.

f. Yes. Parcel post would be ten dollars.

g. Seventeen pounds.

D. More Matching Lines

Match the words.

_c_ **1** bowling

2 wedding

3 crystal punch

a. gift

b. bowl

c. ball

4 unabridged

5 electric

6 toaster

d. oven

e. dictionary

f. toaster

E. Open Road!

You're sending a package. Complete the conversation any way you wish.

A. I'd like to mail this package to ....

B. How would you like to send it?

A. First class, please.

B. Okay. Let me see. It's .... pounds, so that'll be $................................ .

A. $................................?

B. Yes. That's a pretty heavy package you've got there.

A. I guess it is. It's (a/an) .... I'm sending to .... How long will it take to get there?

B. About .... days.

A. About .... days? That's fine.

A. What's the Word?

Complete the conversation.

feature	passengers	decision	trips	controls
finest	stereo	particular	CD	installment
write up	point out	reclines	shop around	spread out

A. May I help you?

B. Yes. I'm interested in this car.

A. You have very good taste. This is one of the _____finest_____ **1** cars we have.

B. Really?

A. Yes. Let me _____ **2** some of its special features.

B. Okay.

A. First, notice that the _____ **3** on the dashboard are all computerized.

B. Hmm. I see that.

A. Also, the seat fully _____ **4** so that your _____ **5** can sleep during those long _____ **6**.

B. That's a very nice _____ **7**.

A. I should also point out that an AM-FM _____ **8** radio with _____ **9** player is included.

B. Oh. That's very interesting. Can I ask how much it costs?

A. Of course. This _____ **10** car costs $20,000, and let me mention that we offer a very good _____ **11** plan to help you _____ **12** the payments.

B. I see.

A. Would you like me to _____ **13** an order slip for you?

B. Not right now, thanks. I want to _____ **14** a little more before I make a _____ **15**.

A. The Right Choice

Circle the correct words.

A. What do you want to [doing / **do**]¹ today?

B. I don't know. Do you have any suggestions?

A. What about [**hang out** / ~~hanging out~~]² at the shopping mall?

B. Hmm. I'm not really in the mood to [~~hang out~~ / hanging out]³

at the shopping mall. Any other ideas?

A. Well, what about [playing / play]⁴ basketball?

B. Good idea! We haven't [play / played]⁵ basketball in a long time.

B. Listen

Listen and put a check next to what these people are going to do today.

① ___ They're going to see a movie.
   ✔ They're going to go jogging.

② ___ They're going to go bowling.
   ___ They're going to have a picnic.

③ ___ They're going to play tennis.
   ___ They're going to go to the ballgame.

④ ___ They're going to go fishing.
   ___ They're going to go swimming.

87

A. Wrong Way!

Put the lines in the correct order.

___ I think I'd prefer to go to the Art Museum.

_2_ Good idea. Which one do you want to go to?

_1_ Why don't we go to a museum today?

___ I don't care. Which one would you rather go to?

_4_ Okay. That's fine with me.

_3_ Oh, I don't know. How about going to the Art Museum?
Or we could always go the Museum of Natural History.

B. Matching Lines

Match the expressions that have the same meaning.

_e_ **1** Let's . . .   a. I'd prefer to . . .

_a_ **2** I'd rather . . .   b. I don't really feel like . . .

_f_ **3** It doesn't matter to me.   c. How about . . . ?

_c_ **4** What about . . . ?   d. Good suggestion!

_b_ **5** I'm not really in the mood to . . . e. Why don't we . . . ?

_d_ **6** Good idea!   f. It doesn't make any difference to me.

C. Open Road!

Complete the conversation any way you wish.

A. Let's .... today!

B. Good idea! (What/Where) ....?

A. Oh, I don't know. How about ....?

   Or we could ....

B. It doesn't matter to me. What would you rather do?

A. I think I'd rather ....

B. Okay. That's fine with me.

D. Listen

Listen and circle what these people are going to do today.

1 ride their bikes (take a hike) **4** play hopscotch play "hide and seek "

2 go bowling stay home **5** visit a museum see a film

3 watch TV go to the movies **6** go skating have a picnic

E. What's the Line?

Complete the conversations with the correct verb forms.

play/playing	see/seeing	ride/riding	take/taking	swim/swimming
have/having	go/going	visit/visiting	do/doing	drive/driving

1

Do you feel like __driving__ to the beach?

I think I'd prefer to __ride__ our bikes.

2

What do you want to _____ today?

How about _____ the new Disney film?

3

Do you have any suggestions?

Yes. Let's __play__ hopscotch.

I'd rather __playing__ "hide and seek."

4

How about __taking__ the kids to the zoo? Or we could __take__ a picnic.

Anything is fine with me.

5

Let's go __swim__ today!

Good idea. Where do you want to go?

It doesn't make any difference to me. How about __going__ to the town pool?

6

Which museum do you want to go to?

How about __visiting__ the Art Museum?

I'd rather __visit__ to the Basketball Museum.

89

Extend Invitations

A. The Right Choice

Circle the correct words.

A. Would you be interested in ((taking) take)[1] a ride in the country tomorrow?

B. (I love to   I'd love to)[2]. I (have taken   haven't taken)[3] a ride in the country in a long time. But wait a minute. Isn't it (suppose to   supposed to)[4] snow tomorrow?

A. Gee. (I hadn't heard   I don't hear)[5] that.

B. I'm pretty sure it's going to snow. They (told   said)[6] so on TV.

A. In that case, (taking   take)[7] a ride probably (would   wouldn't)[8] be a good idea.

B. Hmm. I guess (you're   your)[9] right.

A. Let's wait and see what the weather (be   is)[10] like tomorrow.

B. Okay. I'll call you in the morning.

B. Sense or Nonsense?

Do the following "make sense" or are they "nonsense"?

		Sense	Nonsense
1	"I heard it on the morning news."	✓	
2	"I read it in the paper."	✓	
3	"I watched it on the radio."		✓
4	"The weather forecaster on TV predicted it."	✓	
5	"It rained on the morning news."		✓

C. Listen

Listen and choose the best activity based on the weather.

1 a. Playing tennis is a good idea.
    (b.) Going bowling is a good idea.

2 a. Playing golf sounds like fun.
    b. Going skating sounds like fun.

3 a. Going skiing would be fun.
    b. Seeing a movie would be fun.

4 a. Going sailing is a good idea.
    b. Going sailing isn't a good idea.

5 a. Staying home sounds great.
    b. Driving around the city sounds great.

6 a. Playing football is a good suggestion.
    b. Going to the beach is a good idea.

Decline Invitations

A. What's the Meaning?

Choose the answer that is the closest in meaning.

1 "Would you by any chance be interested in going to a concert this weekend?"
   a. Do you have to go to a concert this weekend?
   b Would you prefer to go to a concert this weekend?
   c. Do you want to go to a concert this weekend?

2 "I'm afraid I won't be able to go. I have to take care of my friend's children."
   a. I can't go because I've got to do something else.
   b. My friend's children won't be able to go.
   c. I'm afraid I won't be able to take care of my friend's children.

3 "Going out for dinner sounds like more fun than attending a business meeting."
   a. Attending business meetings is better than going out for dinner.
   b. I'd rather go out for dinner than attend a business meeting.
   c. I recommend going to business meetings.

B. The Right Choice

Which activities belong in each of these categories?

1 **Indoor Recreation**
   ____ driving to the beach
   ✔ seeing a play
   ✔ going to a museum
   ____ playing golf

2 **Water Activities**
   ____ having a picnic
   ____ roller skating
   ____ swimming
   ____ fishing

3 **Games You Play with a Ball**
   ____ soccer
   ____ tennis
   ____ hockey
   ____ basketball

4 **Outdoor Recreation**
   ____ seeing a play
   ____ taking a hike
   ____ going to a concert
   ____ riding a bike

5 **Children's Activities**
   ____ playing hopscotch
   ____ playing "hide and seek"
   ____ playing golf
   ____ riding a bike

6 **Work Responsibilities**
   ____ hanging out at the mall
   ____ attending a meeting
   ____ writing a report
   ____ visiting a friend

C. Accepted or Rejected?

Did the person accept or reject the invitation?

		Accept	Reject
1	"I'd really like to go skating at the rink."	✓	
2	"I'm sorry. I have to do my homework."		✓
3	"It's foggy, so sailing probably wouldn't be a good idea."	✓	
4	"Hanging out at the shopping mall sounds like fun."	✓	
5	"Watching a comedy sounds like a good idea."		✓
6	"I'm not in the mood to take a hike."		✓
7	"Maybe some other time."		✓
8	"Going on a picnic in the rain wouldn't be very enjoyable."		✓

D. WordRap: *Invitations*

Listen. Then clap and practice.

A. Would you like to come with us?
   We're planning to ski.
B. Sorry. I can't.
   I've got a bad knee.

A. Let's go swimming.
   We'll try the new pool.
B. I'd love to join you,
   But I'm leaving for school.

A. Would you like to go sailing?
   The weather looks great.
B. I'm sorry. I can't.
   I've got a big date!

A. Would you like to have dinner
   With my Uncle Paul?
B. Sorry. I can't.
   I'm expecting a call.

A. Let's make that new recipe.
   I'm dying to try it.
B. I'd really like to,
   But I'm still on my diet.

A. Would you like to watch Fido
   Do a cute little trick?
B. Sorry. I can't.
   I'm feeling sick.

Tell About Weekend Activities

A. The Right Choice

Circle the correct words.

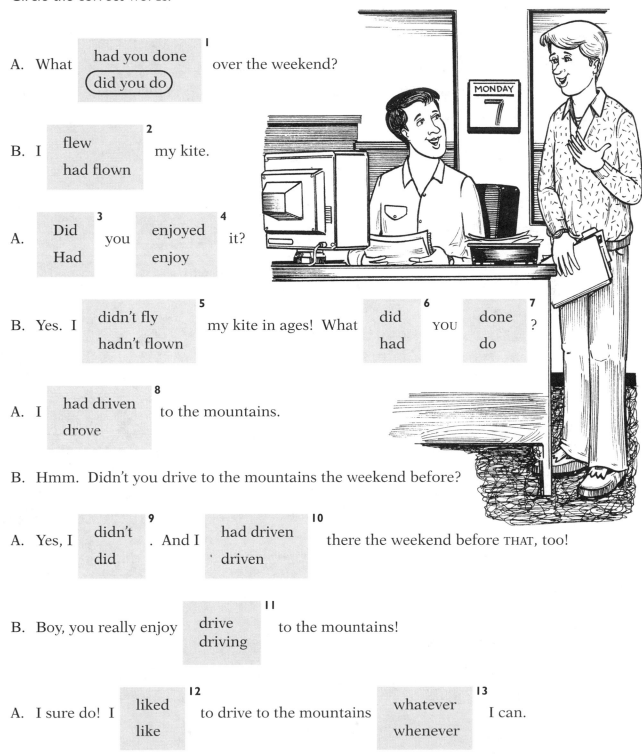

A. What $\begin{array}{c} \text{had you done} \\ \boxed{\text{did you do}} \end{array}$ [1] over the weekend?

B. I $\begin{array}{c} \text{flew} \\ \text{had flown} \end{array}$ [2] my kite.

A. $\begin{array}{c} \text{Did} \\ \text{Had} \end{array}$ [3] you $\begin{array}{c} \text{enjoyed} \\ \text{enjoy} \end{array}$ [4] it?

B. Yes. I $\begin{array}{c} \text{didn't fly} \\ \text{hadn't flown} \end{array}$ [5] my kite in ages! What $\begin{array}{c} \text{did} \\ \text{had} \end{array}$ [6] YOU $\begin{array}{c} \text{done} \\ \text{do} \end{array}$ [7] ?

A. I $\begin{array}{c} \text{had driven} \\ \text{drove} \end{array}$ [8] to the mountains.

B. Hmm. Didn't you drive to the mountains the weekend before?

A. Yes, I $\begin{array}{c} \text{didn't} \\ \text{did} \end{array}$ [9] . And I $\begin{array}{c} \text{had driven} \\ \text{driven} \end{array}$ [10] there the weekend before THAT, too!

B. Boy, you really enjoy $\begin{array}{c} \text{drive} \\ \text{driving} \end{array}$ [11] to the mountains!

A. I sure do! I $\begin{array}{c} \text{liked} \\ \text{like} \end{array}$ [12] to drive to the mountains $\begin{array}{c} \text{whatever} \\ \text{whenever} \end{array}$ [13] I can.

B. Fill It In!

Fill in the correct answer.

1 Dan didn't go to the mall last Sunday because _____.
    (a.) he had gone there on Friday
    b. he hadn't gone there on Friday

2 I enjoyed wearing a tuxedo to the wedding because _____.
    a. I had worn a tuxedo in ages
    b. I hadn't worn a tuxedo in ages

3 I washed my windows last week because _____.
    a. I hadn't washed them in ages
    b. I had washed them in ages

4 I decided to volunteer at my son's school because _____.
    a. I hadn't volunteered before
    b. I had volunteered before

5 Gary got into a motorcycle accident last week because _____.
    a. he had ridden in four years
    b. he hadn't ridden in four years

6 Susan rejected Bill's invitation to see the play because _____.
    a. she had already seen it
    b. she hadn't seen it

C. What's the Response?

Choose the correct response.

1 Did you see the ballgame on TV last night?
    a. Yes. I didn't see a ballgame in ages.
    (b.) Yes. I hadn't seen a ballgame in ages.

2 Is it true you read three novels last week?
    a. Yes. That's because I had had time to read a long time.
    b. Yes. That's because I hadn't had time to read in a long time.

3 Peter looked nauseous when I saw him yesterday afternoon.
    a. He had eaten too much candy for lunch.
    b. He hadn't eaten too much candy for lunch.

D. Listen

Listen and circle the word you hear.

1	wash	(watch)	**6**	done	gone	**11**	made	baked
2	written	ridden	**7**	seemed	seen	**12**	play	skate
3	hurt	heard	**8**	flown	known	**13**	drove	told
4	sent	send	**9**	hiked	biked	**14**	bought	got
5	said	read	**10**	wanted	gotten	**15**	done	drawn

A. What Are They Saying?

Complete the conversation.

A. Did you know that my husband and I won the lottery last year?

B. You (*predict*) _____had been predicting_____ [1] you would win for ages! That's fantastic!

A. I know, but I can't believe it finally happened.

B. What did you do with your lottery winnings?

A. First, my husband and I went to Antarctica. We (*think*) _____ [2] about going there for a long time.

B. Did you enjoy it?

A. It was incredible! We (*expect*) _____ [3] it to be exciting, but it was better than we had anticipated.

B. That's great. Tell me, what else did you do with your winnings?

A. We bought a new house. We (*want*) _____ [4] to buy one for years.

B. That's wonderful.

A. Oh, and I almost forgot to tell you. We took our children on a trip to South America. They (*hope*) _____ [5] to go to South America their whole lives.

B. Did you have a good time?

A. We had a wonderful trip!

B. Listen

Listen and decide what these people are talking about.

1 a. a cruise
   b. a bus trip

2 a. dinner at home
   b. dinner at a restaurant

3 a. a plane ride
   b. a train ride

4 a. a vacation
   b. a picnic

5 a. a trip to the beach
   b. a dance

6 a. a TV program
   b. a movie

95

Use the Newspaper to Make Movie Plans

A. What's the Response?

Choose the correct response.

1. Would you like to see a movie tonight?
   a. Sure.
   b. *The Cowboy Story*.

2. What would you like to see?
   a. What about a comedy?
   b. What's an adventure?

3. How about *A Journey into Space*?
   a. Do you want to see a movie?
   b. *A Journey into Space*?

4. What's it about?
   a. I don't know.
   b. I don't know it.

5. What did the ad in the paper say?
   a. It said, "It's beyond the universe!"
   b. It said it in the paper.

6. Is it a mystery?
   a. Yes. It's a documentary.
   b. No. It's a science fiction movie.

7. Who's in it?
   a. Barbara Burns and Dan Donner.
   b. A science fiction movie.

8. Are you interested?
   a. Sure. I'm interesting.
   b. Sure. I'm interested.

9. What time is it showing?
   a. There are shows at 7 and 9.
   b. It's at the City Cinema.

10. I'd rather go at 7.
    a. That's fine with me.
    b. That's fine to be.

B. Matching Lines

Match the lines.

_d_ 1. City Cinema is proud to present ____.

____ 2. The afternoon shows are at ____.

____ 3. Tickets are $3.00 before ____.

____ 4. Evening tickets cost ____.

____ 5. Thanks for calling ____.

____ 6. The shows this evening are at ____.

____ 7. *El Agua* is this week's special ____.

a. 6:00 in the evening
b. foreign film
c. Fresh Pond Cinema
d. *The Berry Bears*
e. $6.50
f. 1:15 and 3:45
g. 7:15 and 9:45

C. Open Road!

Tell about your favorite kinds of movies.

96

D. Listen

Listen and choose the best name for the movie.

1. **(a.)** *Illnesses of the 21st Century*
   b. *The Great Space War*

2. a. *Lost Love*
   b. *Laugh Time*

3. a. *The Twin Dogs Meet Santa Claus*
   b. *Journey into Deep Space*

4. a. *The Search for the Missing Jewels*
   b. *The Berry Bears Adventure*

5. a. *Agua Caliente*
   b. *Cats and Dogs Everywhere*

6. a. *The French Countryside Today*
   b. *Cowboys on the Run*

E. Crosswalk

What kinds of movies?

1. *The Lost Island*
2. *Toys on Parade*
3. *Asia Today*
4. *Invaders from Mars*
5. *El Hombre*
6. *Good-bye Forever*
7. *Stories of the Old West*
8. *A Time to Laugh*
9. *Dilly Ducks Adventure*
10. *The Missing Watch*

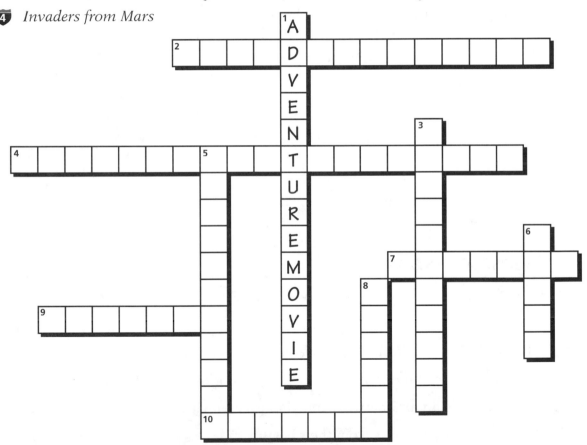

A. The Right Choice

Circle the correct word.

A. What do you want to ((watch)   wash)¹?

B. I don't know. What's (in   on)²?

A. Well, *The Mystery Hour* (is   it's)³ on Channel 7.

B. Oh, I'd rather (not   no)⁴ watch *The Mystery Hour*. I'm tired of
(watch   watching)⁵ that program. What else is on?

A. Well, (there's   it's)⁶ a new miniseries on Channel 6.

B. I'm not really in the (mood   moon)⁷ for a miniseries.
(Do   Are)⁸ you?

A. No, I (guest   guess)⁹ not. How about
(watch   watching)¹⁰ *The Game of Fortune* on Channel 12?
That's supposed to be a pretty good game show.

B. *The Game of Fortune*? I don't know. Maybe we
(must   should)¹¹ watch *The Mystery Hour* after all.

A. It doesn't (difference   matter)¹² to me.

B. Are you sure?

A. Yes. (Whenever   Whatever)¹³ you'd like to watch is fine with me.

B. Sense or Nonsense?

Do the following "make sense" or are they "nonsense"?

		Sense	Nonsense
1	"Going to the movies can be enjoyable."	✓	
2	"People have to stand in line to buy tickets at home."		
3	"A VCR offers an alternative to a night at the movies."		
4	"People can rent movies from their neighbors."		
5	"Watching a movie at home can be convenient."		
6	"VCRs cost about three dollars to buy."		
7	"Some people prefer to rent movies at movie theaters."		
8	"Popcorn is an example of modern technology."		

A. The Right Choice

Circle the correct word.

1. These jeans are too tight. I'd like to try a (smaller (larger)) pair.

2. This briefcase is too heavy. I'd like one that's more (lightweight   powerful).

3. These earrings are too fancy. I'd like to exchange them for more (conservative   difficult) ones.

4. The prices in this catalog are too high. I need to find a catalog with (lower   smaller) prices.

5. Skiing is very expensive. I want to try a (cheaper   larger) sport.

6. The weather here is too cold. I want to live where the weather is (colder   warmer).

B. Matching Lines

Match the lines that have the same meaning.

_d_	1 May I help you?		a. Do you have any ideas?
___	2 Where can I find them?		b. I suppose.
___	3 Do you have any suggestions?		c. I'd rather do that.
___	4 I won't be able to.		d. Can I help you?
___	5 I'd prefer to do that.		e. It doesn't make any difference.
___	6 I'd like to do that.		f. That sounds like fun.
___	7 I guess.		g. Where are they located?
___	8 That sounds great!		h. I want to do that.
___	9 It doesn't matter to me.		i. I can't.

C. Wrong Way!

Put the words in the correct order.

1. a dress bright green   _a bright green dress_

2. a large sweater blue light   _____

3. a beige belt size 34   _____

4. a shirt white press permanent _____

5. a plastic light brown purse   _____

D. Listen

Listen and choose the correct answer.

1. **a.** find one with remote control (circled)
   b. getting one with a large screen

2. a. doing
   b. go

3. a. finding a skirt
   b. look for a blouse

4. a. going to a ballgame
   b. see a play

5. a. cook tonight
   b. washing my car

6. a. exchange them for a bigger pair
   b. returning them

7. a. visiting a museum
   b. go for a drive

8. a. go to the zoo
   b. playing tennis

9. a. work in my garden
   b. reading a novel

10. a. sail
    b. going out to dinner

E. What's the Line?

Complete the sentences.

1. I enjoyed the concert. I (*go*) _____ hadn't gone _____ to a concert in a long time.

2. I loved playing golf last week. I (*play*) _____ golf for several years.

3. I really enjoyed that movie. I (*see*) _____ a movie in ages.

4. We fell when we went roller skating because we (*go*) _____ roller skating in a long time.

5. Fred wore his new tie to work yesterday. He (*wear*) _____ it before.

F. What's the Line?

Complete the sentences.

1. I enjoyed my vacation. I (*plan*) _had been planning_ it for a long time.

2. I was disappointed in the new restaurant. Everyone (*tell*) _____ me how good the food was.

3. The Senior Prom was boring. It's too bad. We (*look forward*) _____ to it all year.

4. We (*hope*) _____ for good weather for our party, and we were lucky! It was sunny and clear.

5. It's a shame you had a miserable vacation. You (*talk*) _____ about your plans for months.

6. I finally had to get a new radiator for my car last week. My old radiator (*leak*) _____ for weeks.

SCRIPTS FOR LISTENING EXERCISES

Page 1

Listen and circle the word you hear.

1. Which apartment do you live in?
2. Who is your supervisor?
3. What floor do you live on?
4. How did you meet them?
5. Whose class is this?
6. Why are you majoring in mathematics?

Page 3

Listen and decide what they're talking about.

1. Does it leave for downtown every fifteen minutes?
2. Who is your supervisor?
3. Whose class are you in?
4. How did you hurt yourself, Mrs. Martinez?
5. Which floor do you live on?
6. Which department do you work in?
7. How do you feel, Mr. Davis?
8. Does it stop in front of the building?
9. How do the neighbors like it here?

Page 4

Listen and choose the correct people.

1. I'd like to introduce my wife and my daughters.
2. These are my parents.
3. This is my nephew.
4. Let me introduce you to my brother and his wife.
5. These are my nieces.
6. I'd like to introduce my mother-in-law.

Page 6

Listen and circle the correct word.

1. When I'm in Florence, I speak . . . .
2. I'm going to Kyoto on vacation to practice my . . . .
3. I'm moving to Stockholm. That's why I'm learning . . . .
4. This is my friend Manuel. He's a . . . .
5. I love to drink Brazilian coffee. I drank it every day when I was in . . . .
6. Seoul is my favorite city in . . . .
7. On my next vacation I'm going to . . . .
8. The national language of Colombia is . . . .
9. In Montreal, people speak English and . . . .

Page 8

Listen and choose the correct response.

1. May I help you?
2. First name Thomas?
3. Are you traveling alone?
4. Are you paying by check?
5. I see here you requested a regular room.
6. How long do you plan to stay?
7. You asked for a room facing the park.
8. My name is George Williston.

Page 13

Listen and decide if it's "good news" or "bad news."

1. I didn't get a promotion!
2. I got a big raise!
3. I flunked my English exam!
4. My daughter graduated from high school last month!
5. Nobody remembered my birthday!
6. I found twenty dollars on the street on my way to work this morning!
7. I got a ticket for speeding today!
8. I left my keys in the house, and now I can't get in!
9. My husband wrecked our new car!
10. Someone took my wallet!

Page 17

Listen and write the number under the correct picture.

1. A. Did the Abro Corporation buy our company?
   B. No. Where did you hear that?
   A. I heard it in the cafeteria.
   B. Well, I can't believe it's true. I'm sure it's just a rumor.
2. A. Can I ask you a question?
   B. Sure. What?
   A. Are the people across the street getting a divorce?
   B. I don't know. Where did you hear that?
   A. All the neighbors are talking about it.
3. A. Are the bus drivers going on strike?
   B. I don't know. Where did you hear that?
   A. Someone mentioned it at the bus stop.
4. A. Did you know that they're going to lay off the workers on the night shift?
   B. Who told you that?
   A. I heard it from the security guard.
   B. Well, I can't believe it's true. I'm sure it's just a rumor.

5. A. Our supervisor wants to shorten our coffee break.
   B. Where did you hear that?
   A. One of the secretaries told me.
   B. Well, I can't believe it's true!
6. A. Did you know that our English teacher was in the 1996 Olympics?
   B. Where did you hear that?
   A. Someone in science class told me.
7. A. I hear that Mrs. Anderson canceled our class picnic.
   B. Really? Where did you hear that?
   A. I heard it in gym class.
   B. Well, I can't believe it's true. I'm sure it's just a rumor.
8. A. Did you know that Santa Claus is just "make believe"?
   B. Who told you that?
   A. One of the girls in my class told me.

Page 21

Listen and number the activities.

1. A. What are you and your husband going to do this weekend?
   B. On Friday evening, we're going to go dancing. On Saturday, we're going to clean out our attic. It's really a mess! And on Sunday, I think we'll go to the beach.
2. A. What are you going to do this weekend?
   B. I'm pretty sure I'll finish my term paper on Friday evening. On Saturday morning, I'll most likely go food shopping. And on Sunday, I'm going to play tennis.
3. A. What's Marge going to do at work today?
   B. First, she'll finish typing a letter for her boss. Then, she'll take a break. And then, she'll go to the post office to mail some packages.
4. A. What are your children going to do this weekend?
   B. They'll most likely go to the movies on Friday evening. On Saturday morning, they're going to clean their rooms. And on Saturday afternoon, I'm going to take them to the circus.

Page 22

Listen and choose the correct response.

1. So, tell me a little about yourself.
2. What do you want to know?
3. I'm originally from Seattle. How about you?
4. Do you still live in Cleveland?
5. Tell me about your family.

6. How about you? Do you have any brothers or sisters?
7. Tell me, what do you do?
8. How about you? What do YOU do?

Page 24

Listen and circle the word you hear.

1. On Friday nights, I like to relax after work.
2. I'm going to take my brother to the theater on Sunday.
3. We'll probably go to a play on Saturday.
4. I'll most likely do chores on Saturday afternoon.
5. Many people have brunch on Sunday.
6. When the weather is nice, I like to take my children to the zoo.
7. Our grandparents are going to visit this weekend.
8. What programs do you like to watch?
9. Do you want to go to a rock concert with me this Saturday evening?

Page 26

Listen and put a check next to the sentence you hear.

1. I hear about it every day.
2. Go to the corner and turn right.
3. I walk to the store every day.
4. Do you have any plans?
5. That telephone number is wrong!
6. She won't go to work tomorrow.
7. That teacher taught math.
8. Sally won the race.

Page 26

Listen and write the spelling of each name.

1. The name is Lawler: L-A-W-L-E-R.
2. The name is Ying: Y-I-N-G.
3. The name is Mills: M-I-L-L-S.
4. The name is Potsky: P-O-T-S-K-Y.
5. The name is Gomez: G-O-M-E-Z.
6. The name is Jarvis: J-A-R-V-I-S.

Page 32

Look at the map and listen to the directions. If the directions are correct, write C. If they are incorrect, write I.

1. A. Do you know how to get to the movie theater?
   B. Sure. Go up Main Street three blocks and turn right onto Second Avenue. Walk along Second Avenue, and you'll see the movie theater on the left, at the intersection of Second Avenue and Park Street.
   A. Thank you very much.
2. A. Excuse me. Is there a laundromat around here?
   B. Yes. There's a laundromat on Third Avenue. Go along Fifth Avenue two blocks. Turn left

onto Center Street. Walk two blocks. You'll see the laundromat on the right, at the intersection of Center Street and Third Avenue.
   A. Thanks.
3. A. Excuse me. I'm looking for the bank. Can you help me?
   B. Sure. Follow Fifth Avenue to Middle Street. Turn right on Middle Street and walk two blocks. You'll see the bank across from City Hall.
   A. Thank you.
4. A. Excuse me. Where's the City Zoo?
   B. The zoo? Hmm. Let me see. Follow Fifth Avenue to Park Street. You'll see the zoo on your left, at the intersection of Park Street and Fifth Avenue.
   A. Thank you very much.
5. A. Is there a hospital nearby?
   B. Yes. Walk up Main Street two blocks. Take a left on Third Avenue. Follow Third Avenue to Middle Street. You'll see the hospital on your right.
   A. Thanks.
6. A. Excuse me. I'm looking for a supermarket. Can you help me?
   B. Sure. Walk along Fifth Avenue to Center Street. Turn left on Center Street and walk two blocks. You'll see the supermarket on the corner, across from the fire station.
   A. Thank you very much.
7. A. Pardon me. Is there a parking lot nearby?
   B. Yes. Go up Main Street one block. You'll see a parking lot on the right, near the police station.
   A. Thanks.
8. A. Could you possibly tell me how to get to the bus station?
   B. Uh-húh. The bus station is right over there, at the intersection of Middle Street and Fifth Avenue.
   A. Oh, thanks. I see it.
9. A. Pardon me. Do you know how to get to the library?
   B. Yes. Walk up Main Street two blocks. You'll see the library on your right, at the intersection of Main Street and Third Avenue.
   A. Thank you.

Page 36

Listen to the traffic report and choose the correct answers.

1. This is Ned Green, your TV 5 traffic reporter, with a rush hour traffic report. There's an accident on Highway 12 near Exit 15. The traffic is stopped. Commuters should take the subway to get to work.

2. Good morning, WCBY listeners. There's an accident on the subway this morning. The trains are very slow and crowded. Commuters should try to hail a cab to get to work.
3. This is the WSDK evening rush hour report. It's snowing, and the trains and buses are late. Getting home from work will be difficult tonight.
4. Today WRTD has some good news for commuters. The new subway system is open! Commuters can ride underground on comfortable new trains.

Page 37

Listen and circle the word you hear.

1. We went to Peru for our vacation.
2. My son-in-law wrecked my new car!
3. For directory assistance, dial 411.
4. Your directions were excellent. I found your house easily.
5. I overheard some people say the boss fired his secretary!
6. My husband left our son at school.
7. I'm sorry, but all of your flowers died!
8. I can't believe it's true!
9. I didn't go to the hospital.
10. Which apartment did you rent?
11. I heard it in the cafeteria.
12. The teacher gave us a lot of homework.

Page 40

Listen and circle the word you hear.

1. I'd like a three-bedroom apartment.
2. Is there anything available downtown?
3. We can't pay more than $560.
4. That includes everything except electricity.
5. Are pets allowed?
6. The neighborhood is very quiet.
7. I'd like a washer and dryer.
8. Are utilities included in the rent?
9. Is the apartment near a bus line?
10. I need an apartment within walking distance of the university.
11. The neighborhood is very convenient.
12. That includes everything except health club dues.

Page 41

Listen and choose the correct response.

1. Could you do me a favor?
2. Could you run over to the store? We need a few things.
3. What do you want me to get?
4. Could you pick up some milk?
5. How many bananas do we need?
6. How much cheese do you want me to get?
7. Is that everything?

8. How much tuna fish should I get?
9. What should we buy to drink?
10. Do we need any toothpaste?
11. How much mayonnaise do you want?
12. Do we have any ice cream in the refrigerator?

Page 44

Listen and choose the correct line to complete the conversation.

1. A. Cheese is in the Dairy Section, Aisle A.
   B. I'm sorry. Did you say Aisle A?
2. A. You can find bug spray in Household Supplies, Aisle G.
   B. Did you say Aisle G?
3. A. Excuse me. Where can I find apple cider?
   B. Look in the Produce Section, Aisle 5.
   A. I'm sorry. Did you say Aisle 9?
4. A. Taco shells are in the Imported Foods Section, Aisle C.
   B. Aisle C?
5. A. Where can I find toothpicks?
   B. They're in Aisle M.
   A. I'm sorry. Did you say Aisle N?
6. A. Lamb chops are with the Frozen Foods, Aisle 7.
   B. Aisle 7?

Page 46

Listen and circle the correct price.

1. That comes to $12.50.
2. The total is $10.54.
3. Your change is $2.40.
4. That'll be $6.76.
5. That comes to $12.25.
6. The total is $30.13.
7. That'll be $1.99.
8. Your change is $.90.
9. That comes to $3.80.
10. The total is $1.17.

Page 48

Do you remember the ingredients of the foods on student text page 68? Listen and write the number under the correct food.

1. A. This is delicious! What's in it?
   B. Let's see . . . a few eggs, a little flour, a little Italian cheese, and a little tomato sauce.
2. A. These are fantastic! What's in them?
   B. Let me see . . . a little pork, a little cabbage, and a few bean sprouts.
3. A. This is excellent! What's in it?
   B. Let me think . . . a little water, a few beets, a little sour cream, and a few onions.
4. A. This is wonderful! What's in it?
   B. Let me see . . . a few eggplants, a few mushrooms, a little ground beef, and a little tomato sauce.
5. A. These are superb! What's in them?

B. Let me think . . . a little flour, a little cheese, a few tomatoes, and a little ground beef.

Page 53

Listen and circle the word you hear.

1. The employees wore their new uniforms yesterday.
2. I write reports in my present job.
3. I've already made seven sandwiches.
4. We've already spoken to our supervisor.
5. Have you met the new employee yet?
6. I eat in the new cafeteria every day.
7. She's already done her work.
8. Has the supervisor seen Michael's letter of resignation yet?
9. Did the clerks take inventory last week?

Page 55

These people are talking at a high school reunion. Listen and put a check next to the things they've done.

A. Hello, George.
B. Oh hi, Jennifer. It's great to see you.
A. Good to see you, too. Tell me, George, what have you done since we finished high school?
B. Well, I've done a lot of things. I've written several books, I've been a counselor at a Family Service Center, and I've traveled to many different countries.
A. That's wonderful. It sounds like you've done a lot of interesting things.
B. How about you, Jennifer? What have YOU done since we finished high school?
A. Well, I've been busy, too. I've studied the piano, I've given ballet lessons, and I've even sung with a rock band.
B. That sounds great, Jennifer.

Page 56

Listen and circle the word you hear.

1. Barbara has taken ballet lessons since 1993.
2. Have you ever flown an airplane?
3. You haven't gone to the bank yet.
4. My daughter hasn't ridden a horse since she was a teenager.
5. Robert has already written his letter of resignation.
6. Have you ever been to London?

Page 58

Which sentence do you hear?

1. A. Can you use the Internet?
   B. Yes, I can. I've been using the Internet since 1995.
2. A. Do you know how to bake?
   B. Yes, I do. I've been baking for years.

3. A. Is Carla busy?
   B. Yes. She's been feeding the animals all morning.
4. A. Is your son able to prepare salads and omelettes?
   B. Yes. He's been preparing them for more than five years.
5. A. Do your parents like Florida?
   B. They love it! They've been living there for a year.
6. A. Have I been talking on the telephone too long?
   B. Well, you've been talking for an hour.

Page 60

Listen to each person's work history, and put a check next to the correct information.

1. In my present job, I've been doing engine tune-ups. And while I haven't changed tires in my current job, I changed tires in the job I had before that.
2. In my present job, I've been selling furniture. And while I haven't sold refrigerators in my current position, I sold refrigerators in the job I had before that.
3. In my present job, I've been writing news stories. And while I haven't written obituaries in my current position, I wrote obituaries in the job I had before that.
4. In my present job, I've been taking inventory. And while I haven't driven the delivery van in my current position, I drove the delivery van in the job I had before that.

Page 61

Listen to the interviews. What did each job applicant do wrong?

1. A. Good afternoon, Mr. Smally. Please sit down.
   B. Thank you.
   A. I see you worked as an office manager for three years. Could you tell me about your responsibilities?
   B. I had a lot of responsibilities. They were very difficult, and I quit the job.
   A. What kinds of responsibilities did you have?
   B. You know, I can't remember them very well.
2. A. Good morning, Ms. Short. Your interview was scheduled for 10:15, and it's now 11:30.
   B. I know, but I slept late. I'm sorry I wasn't able to be here on time.
   A. Well, Ms. Short, punctuality is very important in this company.
   B. I promise I'll never be late again.

3. A. Good afternoon, Mr. Curtis. It's nice to meet you.
   B. Nice to meet you, too. I'd like you to meet my brother Albert and my cousin Marvin. They came with me for the interview.
   A. Oh, I see.
4. A. Please sit down, Ms. Jackson.
   B. Thank you. Excuse me, Mr. Moody, but do you by any chance have any gum? I can't find mine.
   A. I'm afraid I don't, Ms. Jackson. I never chew gum.

Page 63

Listen and choose the next line of the conversation.

1. My dishwasher has flooded the kitchen!
2. Grandpa has just fallen down the stairs, and he can't walk!
3. A fire has broken out in the building on the corner!
4. A robber has just crawled through a window of my apartment!
5. There's been a strange animal noise in the fireplace all morning!
6. I think Aunt Louise has just had a heart attack!

Page 65

Listen and choose the correct answer.

1. Decongestant spray is in Aisle E, on the middle shelf.
2. The dry skin lotion you're looking for is in Aisle B, near the pharmacy.
3. Medicine for a stomachache is in the middle of Aisle D, across from the decongestant spray.
4. Medicine for a backache is in Aisle A, on the first shelf.
5. Eyedrops? Let me see . . . They're in Aisle C, on the middle shelf.
6. Cough medicine is in Aisle A, on the third shelf, next to the pharmacy.
7. Headache tablets are located in Aisle C, on the first shelf, just before the eyedrops.
8. Hair spray is located in the back of the store, next to the pharmacy.

Page 67

Listen and choose the sentence to finish the conversation.

1. I've had a headache for several days.
2. Our dog Bozo has been nauseous since yesterday.
3. All the people in the office have itchy, watery eyes.
4. My husband has had a terrible toothache since last night.
5. My daughter has a bad earache.
6. My skin has been very dry all winter.
7. Our cat hasn't been able to move

her leg since she jumped out of a tree last Sunday.
8. A man in my apartment building fell down the stairs and hasn't been able to move his shoulder for three days.
9. There's been a bad accident on the expressway!
10. The elderly woman in Apartment 4G has had a heart attack!

Page 70

Listen and choose the sentence that is closest in meaning.

1. You should join an organization that helps people "kick the habit."
2. I strongly recommend that you cut back on your responsibilities.
3. It's essential for you to change your eating habits.
4. It might be a good idea to find a hobby that you like.
5. You have to begin an exercise routine.
6. I strongly urge you to eat less salty food.

Page 71

Listen and circle the word you hear.

1. Why don't they try warm milk with honey?
2. They've been nauseous for three days.
3. They're supposed to take the medicine every four hours.
4. When is their appointment?
5. They'll start eating less salty food next week.
6. They've tried home remedies for minor illnesses.

Page 75

Listen and choose the best response.

1. Could you do me a favor?
2. I'm confident I'd be able to sell computers.
3. It's amazing how little you can buy these days for $10.00!
4. I don't want to make manicotti for dinner. Do you have any other ideas?
5. You're supposed to set the tables by 11:00 o'clock.
6. Do you think you'll be able to type the letters today?
7. So, the apartment has two bedrooms and is $850 a month?
8. Do you have any suggestions about my back problems?

Page 76

Listen and put a check next to the sentence you hear.

1. Dishwashers are on "9."
2. Returns are at the rear of the store.
3. Gloves are near the side entrance.
4. Women's shoes are in Aisle G.

Page 79

Listen and circle the product the customer wants to buy.

1. I'd like the one with a self-cleaning oven.
2. I want the one that's also a calculator.
3. I need the one with 16 megabytes of memory.
4. I'd like the one with the 25-inch screen and remote control.
5. I want the one that makes 8 cups and beeps when it's ready.
6. I'd like the one with an automatic ice maker.

Page 81

Listen and choose the best response.

1. I bought a new color TV last night.
2. This is my new bedroom set.
3. Look at these jeans.
4. I got a black purse for the dance next weekend.
5. I want to buy a new car.
6. My son needs a pair of new sneakers.
7. I'm going to buy a coffeemaker.
8. I really like this sweater.
9. We're interested in a gas range.
10. We're looking for a sofa.

Page 83

Listen and choose the best response.

1. I'd like to return these gloves. They're too dark.
2. This VCR is too difficult to operate.
3. Let's return this necktie. It's too conservative.
4. I don't want this sofa. It's too big.
5. That coffeemaker only makes 4 cups. It's too small.
6. This shortwave radio is too weak.
7. I want to exchange this coat for a shorter one.
8. The prices in this store are too high.

Page 84

Listen and choose the correct answer.

Conversation 1

A. I'd like to mail this package to Houston.
B. How would you like to send it?
A. First class, please.
B. Okay. It's seven pounds, so that's eleven dollars and sixty-nine cents.
A. Eleven sixty-nine?
B. Well, it could be sent parcel post, if you want. It would be eight dollars and seventy-five cents. It'll take about ten days.
A. Okay. I'll send it parcel post.

Conversation 2

A. I'd like to mail this package to Miami.

B. How would you like to send it?
A. First class, please.
B. Okay. It's twelve pounds, so that's ten dollars and thirty-one cents.
A. Ten thirty-one? Would it be cheaper to send it parcel post?
B. Oh, yes. Parcel post to Miami is five eighty-nine.
A. Will it take longer to get there?
B. Yes. It'll take about a week.
A. Hmm. It's a wedding present, and the wedding is this Saturday. I'd better send it first class.

Page 87

Listen and put a check next to what these people are going to do today.

1. A. What do you want to do today?
   B. How about seeing a movie?
   A. Hmm. I don't feel like seeing a movie. Any other ideas?
   B. How about going jogging?
   A. Good idea. We haven't gone jogging in a long time.
2. A. How about having a picnic today?
   B. I'm not really in the mood for a picnic. How about going bowling?
   A. Good idea! We haven't gone bowling in a long time.
3. A. What do you feel like doing today?
   B. I'm in the mood to play tennis.
   A. Hmm. I don't really want to play tennis. Any other suggestions?
   B. We could go to the ballgame.
   A. Good idea!
4. A. What about going swimming today?
   B. I'm not really in the mood to go swimming. How about going fishing?
   A. Good idea! We haven't gone fishing in a long time.

Page 89

Listen and circle what these people are going to do today.

1. Let's go for a walk in the mountains today!
2. I don't feel like playing tennis. I'd prefer to go bowling.
3. Let's go to an adventure movie!
4. Come on, Bobby! Let's play "hide and seek!"
5. Let's get together this weekend. I'd like to go to a museum.
6. How about packing a lunch and going to the lake?

Page 90

Listen and choose the best activity based on the weather.

1. It's going to be very cold and windy today.
2. The weather tomorrow will be warm and sunny.
3. It'll be rainy and warm tomorrow, with a chance of a little sunshine in the afternoon.
4. It's foggy today, so be careful driving!
5. There are several inches of snow predicted for the metropolitan area tomorrow.
6. It's 85 degrees today, and tomorrow will be even warmer!

Page 94

Listen and circle the word you hear.

1. Did you watch the weather forecast?
2. I got a letter from my cousin yesterday. She hadn't written in a long time.
3. My dog was hurt in an accident.
4. He didn't send any money in the package.
5. I said this car costs $15,000.
6. No, I hadn't gone to the beach the weekend before.
7. I hadn't seen her in ages.
8. Phillip has never flown before.
9. We went to the mountains last week. We hadn't hiked since last summer.
10. We had wanted to play golf, but the weather was bad.
11. Have you ever made sushi?
12. Why don't we skate at the lake?
13. Who drove you to the movie?
14. I wanted to go skiing last weekend, but I hadn't bought skis yet.
15. She had drawn some beautiful pictures.

Page 95

Listen and decide what these people are talking about.

1. A. The truth is, we didn't have a very good time. The water was choppy, and our cabins were very small.
   B. That's too bad. You had been looking forward to it for a long time.
2. A. Did you enjoy it?
   B. Not really. The food was terrible, and the service was slow.
   A. I'm sorry to hear that. You had been talking about going there for weeks!
3. A. How was it?
   B. It was awful! The ride was bumpy, and they showed a movie I had already seen.
4. A. Did you have a good time?
   B. Not really. The hotel was crowded, and the weather was miserable.
   A. That's a shame. You had been looking forward to it for a long time.
5. A. Did you have a good time?
   B. Not really. The band was too loud, and they played very old-fashioned music.
6. A. How was it?
   B. I didn't enjoy it very much. It was very boring, and we had terrible seats.
   A. That's too bad. You had really been looking forward to seeing it.

Page 97

Listen and choose the best name for the movie.

1. City Cinema is proud to present a new documentary about health problems. Showing daily at 8 and 10 P.M.
2. Thank you for calling the Mall Cinema. We have a new feature film. It's a comedy starring Gene Little and Sally Gold. Come and see it daily at 7 and 9 P.M.
3. Bring the kids to the East Town Mall Cinema to see a new computer-generated cartoon about two lovable animals. Showing every afternoon at 1 and 3 P.M.
4. The West Town Mall Cinema is featuring a new children's film starring everybody's favorite bears. Shows are daily at 2 and 4 P.M.
5. Join us for a foreign adventure at the Downtown Cinema every day at 5 and 7 P.M.
6. The Baker Theater is proud to present a new western starring Bill Blades and Emily Rose. Shows are at 7:30 and 9:45 daily.

Page 100

Listen and choose the correct answer.

1. If you buy a TV, you should . . . .
2. Where do you want to . . . ?
3. Can you help me . . . ?
4. How about . . . ?
5. I don't feel like . . . .
6. These gloves are too small. I'd like to . . . .
7. I'm not really in the mood to . . . .
8. Why don't we . . . ?
9. I'd rather . . . .
10. Would you by any chance be interested in . . . ?

CORRELATION
ExpressWays Student Text/Activity Workbook

Student Text Pages	Activity Workbook Pages	Student Text Pages	Activity Workbook Pages
Exit 1		**Exit 6**	
2–7	1–3	94–95	63
8–9	4	96–97	64
10–11	5–6	98–99	65
12–13	7–8	100–101	66–67
14–17	9–12	102–103	68–69
		104–105	70
Exit 2		106–109	71–72
20–23	13–15	110–111	73
24–27	16–18		
28–29	19–21	**Exit 7**	
30–33	22–24	116–117	76–77
		118–119	78–79
Exit 3		120–121	80–81
36–37	25–26	122–125	82–83
38–39	27–28	126–129	84–85
40–43	29–30	130–131	86
44–47	31–33		
48–51	34–36	**Exit 8**	
		134–135	87
Exit 4		136–137	88–89
56–59	39–40	138–139	90
60–63	41–42	140–141	91–92
64–65	43–44	142–143	93–94
66–67	45–46	144–145	95
68–69	47–48	146–147	96–97
70–73	49–50	148–151	98
Exit 5			
76–77	51		
78–79	52–53		
80–81	54–55		
82–83	56		
84–85	57		
86–87	58–59		
88–89	60		
90–91	61–62		